WATER GARDEN PROJECTS
FROM GROUNDWORK TO PLANTING

A view of Sir Peter Miller's garden,
Sark, Channel Islands

WATER GARDEN PROJECTS

FROM GROUNDWORK TO PLANTING

Roger Sweetinburgh

GUILD OF MASTER CRAFTSMAN PUBLICATIONS LTD

First published 2002 by
Guild of Master Craftsman Publications Ltd
Castle Place, 166 High Street,
Lewes, East Sussex BN7 1XU

ISBN 1 86108 292 4

Cover design by Ian Smith
Cover photographs: GMC Publications/Ed Gabriel

Colour origination by Viscan Graphics (Singapore)
Printed in China by Sun Fung Offset Binding Co Ltd

CONTENTS

* This article first appeared in *Exotic & Greenhouse Gardening* magazine

INTRODUCTION

There has always been a place for water in the garden, and years ago this would usually have been a pond with some goldfish. Now, with the advent of butyl liners, a good selection of affordable pumps and the wide choice of water features offered by most garden centres, the idea of having some water in the garden has never been so appealing.

This book is full of delightfully creative self-build projects designed to give your garden a touch of individuality. Some are traditional ideas which have been redesigned so that they work reliably year in, year out, while others are quite novel yet easy to build. Each project is described with the help of stunning full-colour illustrations and clear, easy-to-follow text based on the author's extensive practical experience, so that anyone with only basic do-it-yourself skills can produce an attractive and, above all, reliable water feature.

Included in these projects are details about pumps and various types of fountain, how to make a whole range of cascades and how to install wall-mounted water features. There are various ideas on how to attract wildlife to an existing pond, how to create a 'natural' water feature from scratch and how to keep out unwanted visitors. Other projects include how to build a raised pond, install an area of decking over some water, build a grotto and various other unusual features.

Although many of the projects are on a relatively small scale, the principles behind them can easily be applied to much larger projects, making this book useful to landscape contractors and students, and anyone else who wants to create truly *reliable* water features.

PRACTICALITIES
Ponds, Fountains and pumps

Installing a fountain and pump may sound complicated but once the secrets are revealed, it's easy – and well worth the effort

Making

O ver the past few years it is amazing how many new fountains, and pumps, have come onto the market. Most are easy to install but the mass of technical information which seems so often to come with them must put some people off trying them out.

The water feature shown in the drawings consists of two separate pools, possibly made from concrete, with two completely different fountains. Each fountain has its own pump and its own special surroundings. The bell jet fountain is within a circular pool and surrounded by several rounded boulders. There are no significant plants, just stones and water. In sharp contrast, the geyser jet fountain

has been placed within a rock pool and is actually wedged between some rocks in the centre of the pool. A conventional spray fountain could have been used in both situations but probably would not have looked as interesting.

Pump

Beneath every fountain there should be a good pump. The vast majority of these are submersible, which means they operate in the water. They take water in through some sort of built-in or add-on filter, then discharge it through a top pipe. Some fountains will fit directly onto

this top pipe while others are connected using a flexible hose.

Occasionally, surface pumps are used. These operate out of the water in a suitable dry chamber close to the water feature. Ideally, the chamber should be positioned so that the pump can be below the level of the pool or feature. When it is switched off, the pump should then remain full of water. If the pump drains dry when it is

> ❝ *Beneath every fountain there should be a good pump* ❞

waves

switched off, it may have to be primed with some water to get it going again – some surface pumps, however, are self-priming. Being outside the water feature, it will need a pipe to collect the water from the pool and another to deliver it back. Both types of pumps require a properly installed, safe, and weatherproof electricity supply, fitted by a qualified electrician.

Flow valve
The chances of having exactly the right-sized pump always producing exactly the right flow and therefore the perfect size of fountain are not all that great, especially if dirt begins to clog the pump and reduce its efficiency. As a general rule it is a good idea to use a pump which is more powerful than you

need and to add a flow valve. This acts like a volume control enabling you to increase or decrease the flow at will. The flow of a pump with plenty of spare power can then be reduced initially but increased again later as dirt, along with wear, begin to affect efficiency.

Pump performance
Pump performance is usually measured and expressed in litres per hour. The higher a pump has to push water above the level of the pool the lower the

output will be. This distance is known as the 'head'. Performance tables therefore give a range of litres per hour in relation to various heads of water. For most simple fountains the head is reckoned to be about 1m (3.3ft). It will be greater than this for large fountains and probably greater still for high waterfalls. It is also important to remember that the friction created inside a pipe will reduce the flow.

Pump connections

Most pump connections are high quality plastic and very simple to assemble. Larger installations may use metal fittings and a more complex layout.

Although many fountains fit directly onto the top pipe of a submersible pump, this may not necessarily mean that the actual nozzle will be at the correct height above the water. It could also mean that the pump will be right out in the centre of the pond where it could be difficult to reach for maintenance and adjustment. An alternative is to have a fountain stand, which may need fixing down in some way, and a length of flexible pipe connecting it with a pump placed, more conveniently, at the edge of the pool. Most domestic projects are not large enough to warrant this arrangement. Only where a surface pump is being used will a fountain stand almost certainly be necessary.

Clean water

As you might imagine, most fountains work by water passing through small holes or apertures. Dirty water is therefore likely to clog these and prevent the fountain from working properly. Most pumps have a built-in filter of some sort and the more elaborate this is, the longer the fountain will keep working provided that it is cleaned from time to

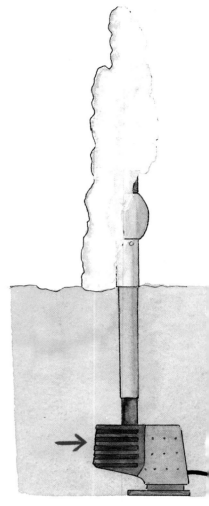

time. In addition to the pump filter you could install an overall filtration system that will clean all the water in the pond. It means having a second pump as well as a tank to disguise, but it should ensure that the pump filter remains largely clear apart from the odd piece of pond weed or water snail.

Spray fountains

The pattern and density of the spray depends upon the size and number of holes in the fountain head, while the spray height depends upon the pump's output. As a rough guide, a medium-sized fountain with a spray pattern up to about 1.5m (5ft) high could need a pump that delivers 3,000 litres per hour. This should be used in conjunction with a flow valve, so that it can be adjusted.

Bell jet fountains

Most bell jet fountains can be adjusted by tightening or loosening a nut or collar on the top of the stem. For a bell about 26cm (10in) across use a pump that delivers 500 litres per hour. For a bell about 40cm (16in) across, use a pump which delivers nearer 1,300 litres per hour. It is especially important to have clean water for a bell jet.

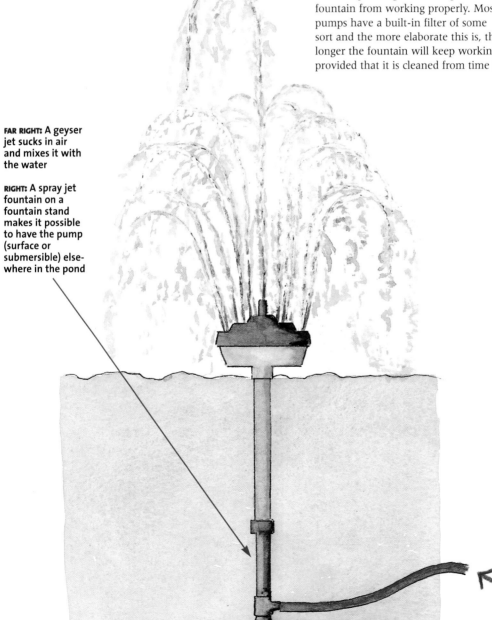

FAR RIGHT: A geyser jet sucks in air and mixes it with the water

RIGHT: A spray jet fountain on a fountain stand makes it possible to have the pump (surface or submersible) elsewhere in the pond

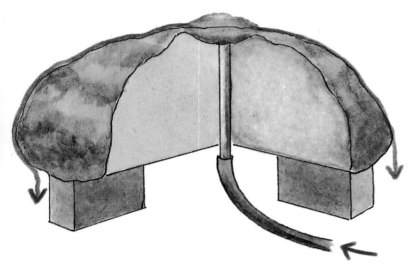

ABOVE: Stones are drilled and fitted with a rigid pipe. A hollowed out area at the top encourages the water to produce a bubbling effect

Geyser or foam jet

The effect that a geyser or foam jet fountain produces can vary from a tall column of foam to a fairly broad cone. It is produced by the jet mixing air with water and can look very effective lit up at night. For a jet about 30cm (12in) high, use a pump which delivers 3,000 litres per hour.

Bubbling stones and boulders

Bubbling stones and boulders have a large surface area to cover so although the actual jet of water should not be too vigorous, the volume of water needed can be quite high – between 1,200 and 5,000 litres per hour depending on the size of the rock. The higher rates often produce a small geyser effect in the hollowed out

section at the top of the stone. This is created by the fact that the jet of water is forcing its way up through a modest depth of water in this hollow.

Ornaments

Most ornaments require only a small flow and can look rather silly if over-powered! Most work well on 600 litres per hour but a flow valve is useful to make sure this is not too much. These performance figures are based on approximately 1m (3.3ft) head of water. If an ornament discharges its water well above this height, above the pool's surface, then the flow needed must be calculated using a correspondingly greater head of water. High waterfalls could involve a head of several metres.

Useful guidelines

■ No fountain should be higher than the radius of its pool or reservoir otherwise water could be lost on a windy day.

■ In the case of spray fountains and geysers the fountain nozzle is held just above the surface of the water. Bell jet fountains are produced from the top of a stem and should come with instructions explaining how far above the water's surface this must be.

■ Nature or 'natural' ponds should generally have still water and therefore no fountain. If a fountain is placed in one of these ponds, it should be quite small so as not to disturb the surface of the water too much. In general, however, fountains help to oxygenate the water which can be beneficial for the fish.

■ The addition of underwater lights can bring any fountain alive at night. There are many different types including some which are designed to clip onto the stem of a fountain.

■ When planning the electrical installation for a pool and fountain, include at least three sockets – one each for the fountain, the lights, and perhaps a pool filter. Where possible, some planting or rocks should be incorporated close to the pool so that electrical sockets can be hidden.

■ It is possible to have pumps and lights turned on and off from the house using a remote control unit. It may also be possible to control the speed, and therefore the output, of the pump remotely. Although most pumps, and some lights, work directly off the full mains voltage, some work from lower voltages through a transformer. This needs to be as close to the pump as possible, housed in a dry, well-ventilated chamber – not in the water – so that there is no significant power loss due to a long cable.

❝ *Most pumps have a built-in filter of some sort and the more elaborate this is the longer the fountain will keep working* ❞

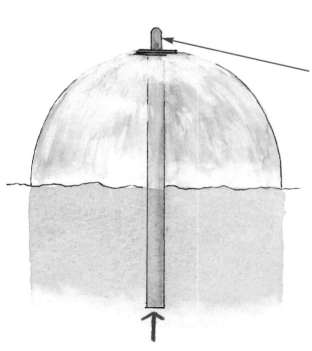

LEFT: A bell jet can usually be adjusted using this top screw

RIGHT: Fountain ornaments have a rigid pipe built into them. A flexible pipe is needed to connect up with the pump

Pumping out the action

How to build problem-free header pools, spillways and cascades

ABOVE: Cascades and pools of varying size and volume add interest to this waterfall

I f ever something has been built badly in a garden it will, more often than not, be the water feature; perhaps swathes of liner will be on display, or a loosely disguised hosepipe will be allowed to serve as a crude fountain or cascade squirting water into the air.

A totally artificial but reasonably natural-looking 'moving' water feature can, however, be created without much extra time and effort; what does take more skill, however, is the devising of a feature which works day in, day out without losing or leaking any of the constantly recycled water to the surrounding garden – for not only are header pools, spillways and cascades the focal point of such a feature, they are also where most water loss occurs.

Pump types

Pumps, of course, make these features 'move'. Most are submersible, staying underwater at the lowest point in the system, drawing water directly into themselves via a small filter, and pushing it along a pipe to wherever it is required.

Surface pumps are used less and must be housed in a dry chamber close to but below the surface level of the lowest pool. They have a pipe which draws water from the pool and another which delivers it as before.

The success of a spillway or cascade depends very much on the pump. A pump's performance will depend upon how far and, above all, how high the water has to be pushed (height = head).

The flow diminishes as the 'head' increases, so this factor must be added when working out pump size. The pump should be up to 50% more powerful than is needed at the appropriate 'head'; then fit a flow valve so that the overall performance and effect can be controlled up or down.

A pump which has to run flat out all the time is likely to perform less well as time goes by, if only because the filter gradually blocks up, leading to wear and tear.

Pump choice

Using the wrong pump can have dire consequences. Imagine switching on a new feature's pump for the first time. Everyone waits for the initial gurgling to translate into a dramatic alpine cascade; instead, a pathetic trickle emerges at the top and makes it way slowly back down to the bottom pool – all because the pump is far too small.

Better that someone has to leap into action to turn down a valve because the water is gushing with such fervour it is in danger of flooding the garden.

Conversely, there is nothing more ridiculous than an urn or a millstone being connected to such a powerful pump that the result is reminiscent of a burst water main.

The Appendix on page 114

ABOVE: Garden stream with tumbling water, small pool and marginal plants

HARRY SMITH COLLECTION

HL PHOTOGRAPHICS

ABOVE: Delicacy of this slight water flow allows the beauty of the slate to come through and a pleasing sound to be heard

"There is nothing more ridiculous than an urn or a millstone being connected to such a powerful pump that the result is reminiscent of a burst water main"

gives some idea of how to calculate the correct pump size.

Bear in mind, too, that the pool or vessel which houses the submersible pump must hold a generous volume of water. It is from here that the water is taken to work the feature, top up all the pools until they overflow, and replace water lost through evaporation and leaks.

If the pool begins to run dry, the pump could start to suck in air and so be damaged. Such a drop in the water level may also look unsightly.

Effects

Setting aside some of the contrived features – lions' heads, squirting toads, millstones and so on – there are clay drainpipes, gullies, streams, waterfalls, holes in walls and many

other natural ways of discharging water.

A narrow bamboo pipe with the discharge end cut at a slant will, for example, deliver a narrow spout of water, but only if a relatively gentle pump is used.

Larger pipes will take a greater volume of water to produce a similar but altogether larger-scale effect.

Natural pieces of rock must be smooth, with a natural or man-made throat under the front edge to help the water fall cleanly rather than dribbling back underneath.

To achieve a full curtain from

ABOVE: Slender outfall adds focus without swamping plantings, but still requires a flow of about 450 litres (100 gallons) per hour

the edge of a rock requires a considerable volume of water and, therefore, a fairly powerful pump.

A flat surface in the form of a slab, tile or some sort of chute must also have a throat or lip and, again, quite a powerful pump to produce a good curtain of water.

Round stones in a small, fast-flowing stream will produce a different sound from angular, sharp stones, and so on.

Foolproof arrangement

A cascade or similar effect created well within an existing watertight system is usually troublefree because, even if there are any unintentional leaks, the water does stay within the overall system.

Add-on features can, on the

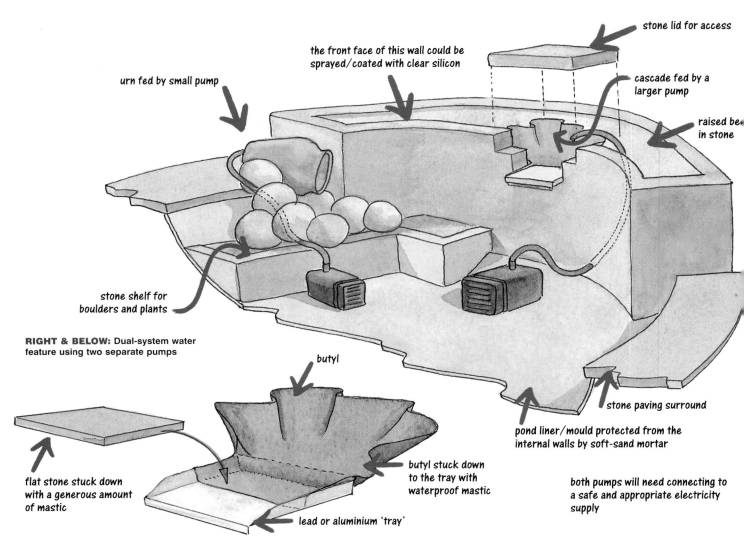

stone lid for access

the front face of this wall could be sprayed/coated with clear silicon

cascade fed by a larger pump

urn fed by small pump

raised be[d] in stone

stone shelf for boulders and plants

RIGHT & BELOW: Dual-system water feature using two separate pumps

butyl

stone paving surround

pond liner/mould protected from the internal walls by soft-sand mortar

flat stone stuck down with a generous amount of mastic

butyl stuck down to the tray with waterproof mastic

both pumps will need connecting to a safe and appropriate electricity supply

lead or aluminium 'tray'

other hand, be troublesome if they cannot deliver water directly into the existing system. A stone trough, for example, would need to be fitted with a pipe or chute before it could discharge water without dribbling and leaking.

An urn is made to pour and so can operate quite well just as it is – but of course with a hole in the back for a delivery pipe.

A rocky spillway or stream coming from somewhere beyond the main system or pond must have a generous overlap into the pool if it is to work well. The raised water feature illustrated shows how an add-on feature can be made to work reliably although, if it did leak, part of it is over the existing pond.

As far as the wall cascade is concerned, water comes directly from a pipe into a small butyl reservoir behind the wall opening. This butyl overlaps into an open-ended tray which has a downturned lip ensuring that

the water flows off in a curtain.

The tray on its own would look odd, so a smooth, flat piece of stone has been stuck down into the tray using a heavy-duty mastic so that virtually all the water flows over the stone, not under it.

The urn is also simple to set up but the two features are on separate pumps because the urn needs a gentle flow and the wall a much more vigorous one.

There is a possibility that the wall could absorb water from the pool – or even from the cascade on a windy day. This can be minimised by using a hard and, therefore, fairly non-absorbent walling stone and by spraying the face of the wall with clear silicone.

The back of the wall could be damp-proofed with bitumastic paint or 'tanking'.

Other ideas

Spillways are often in the form of streams and gullies feeding water in a pool. In an

artificial system the stream has to be built like a long, thin pool – perfectly level, with a slightly lower dam at one end over which the water flows.

The pump may sometimes be switched off but, because of the way it has been constructed, the artificial stream should remain full of water.

In a sloping garden it may be possible to create a series of linked streams, falls and pools, choosing to vary the height of the falls and depths of water rather than making them all the same.

High waterfalls produce a different sound from low ones, and water falling into a deep pool sounds different from water falling into a shallow one.

Where water

is to emerge from a hole or aperture of some description, a gushing effect may be inappropriate, so make sure the delivery pipe is as far back from the outflow point as possible, to allow a full, steady flow to develop before it emerges.

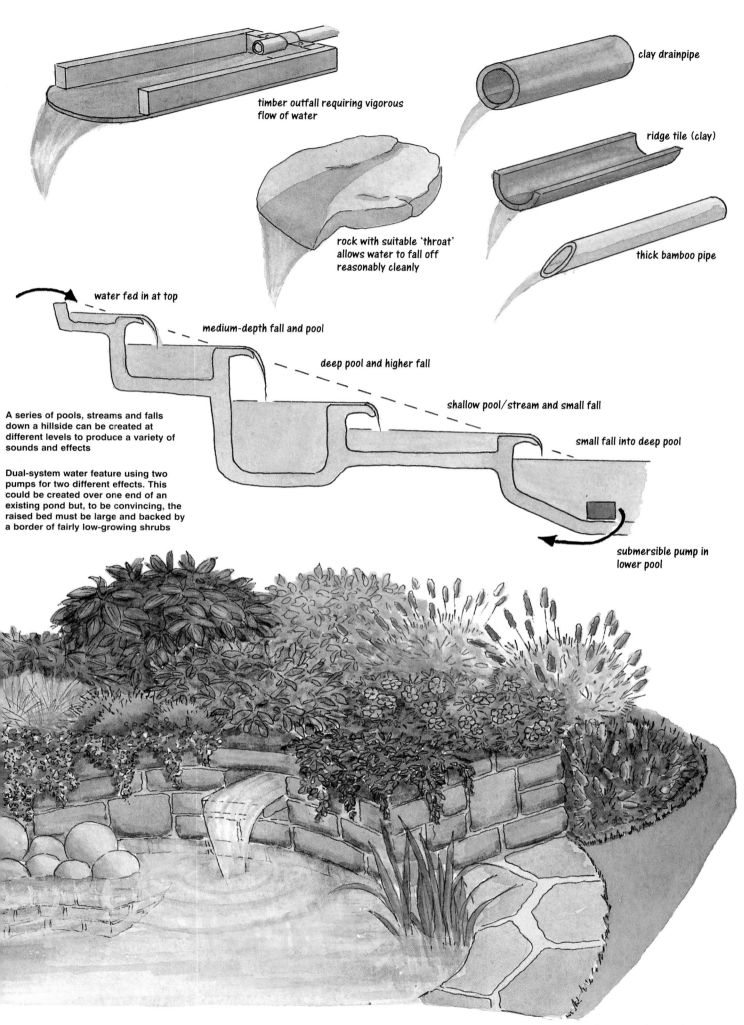

timber outfall requiring vigorous
flow of water

clay drainpipe

ridge tile (clay)

rock with suitable 'throat'
allows water to fall off
reasonably cleanly

thick bamboo pipe

water fed in at top

medium-depth fall and pool

deep pool and higher fall

shallow pool/stream and small fall

small fall into deep pool

A series of pools, streams and falls
down a hillside can be created at
different levels to produce a variety of
sounds and effects

Dual-system water feature using two
pumps for two different effects. This
could be created over one end of an
existing pond but, to be convincing, the
raised bed must be large and backed by
a border of fairly low-growing shrubs

submersible pump in
lower pool

Pumping out the action 11

ABOVE: Primulas and *Erinus alpinus* look spectacular above this cascade

Boosting flow

Many filters work on the principle that water enters the tank briskly through a narrow pipe but comes out through a much wider one. Although the same volume of water comes out as goes in, it flows out at a much more leisurely rate – frustrating for anyone trying to create a gushing stream or waterfall immediately after the filter.

A way around the problem is to have a second pump working alongside the main one in the lowest pool, but delivering water directly to the top of the cascade rather than through the filter.

Changing direction

Where a series of streams or pools are linked together it is customary to have all the cascades facing the same way.

Under some circumstances it is possible to turn the water 90° by making it cascade out from the side of the pool into the next rather than constantly going forwards. This can make the overall effect more interesting and also make it possible to see a 'fall' from somewhere else in the garden.

Splitting supply

As the flow can usually be split, several of the above ideas could be achieved with just one pump. But if one branch is significantly smaller than the other, and the filter begins to block or the pump becomes less efficient, it is all too possible that the weaker of the two flows could cease altogether.

So while initial costs of buying and connecting two pumps are higher, the long-term prospects are often much better if this course is taken.

Calculating pump size

Assuming that the surface over which the water will flow is smooth, the creation of a thin curtain of water just 50mm (2in) wide calls for a minimum flow of about 450 litres (100 gallons) per hour.

A curtain twice that wide requires a flow at least twice as great and if the surface is rough, it will take even more water.

Tables of pump performances state the expected flow output at various heads.

ABOVE: Formal curtain of water slips seemingly effortlessly from one pool to another, but in fact needs a pump of considerable capacity

ABOVE: Message from a bottle

To calculate the pump you need, look for a flow about 50° greater than you need at the maximum head of your water feature.

Along with the pump, purchase a flow restriction valve which is fitted to the outflow pipe. Where pond life or planting is an important feature, avoid vigorous cascades or excessive flow.

ED GABRIEL

Getting rid of VPL

Not many self-respecting ponds are built without a liner, but no-one actually wants to see them. Here are some suggestions for attractive and reliable ways of hiding your Visible Plastic Liner

Many modern ponds are now made using a butyl liner. Books and catalogues usually show a hole being dug in an apparently level area of grass, being lined with butyl and having a row of paving stones laid all around the edge. The end result can look very attractive – if the ground is level to start with – but little mention is made of the possibility that the paved edge, resting on little more than hard soil, could eventually subside into the pond.

Despite frequent rain, the water level in the pond will often drop due to evap-oration, but again little mention is made of what to do about the ugly swathe of butyl which inevitably appears around the edges. There are ways of avoiding both these problems. It may take a little more effort during the construction, and cost a little more, but the end result will be infinitely superior.

ABOVE: Well supported turf and decking surround this Chelsea 2000 pond and disguise its liner

> ❝ *An area of bricks or blocks can look very attractive coming right up to the edge of a pond* ❞

> **The most practical
> way of using real stone
> around curved edges is
> to pave with broken
> pieces**

RIGHT: Informal pool
illustrating the use of various
types of well-supported paving
and showing no visible butyl

Paved edge choice

Brick and block paviors An area of
bricks or blocks can look very attractive
coming right up to the edge of a pond.
They can be cut quite easily and therefore follow the curves of an informal
pond, although it is essential to run
one row of blocks 'end on' around the
edge of the curves to finish off the cut
edges properly.

In the case of brick paving, use only
stock bricks since ordinary house bricks
or 'flettons' are not normally frost
resistant. Bricks are not, in fact,
designed for paving, so if they are to fit
most paving patterns, they must be laid
with mortar joints between.

Brick – and concrete block – paviors,
however, are made specifically for
paving and fit together without the
need for mortar joints. This creates a
rather modern effect so if the property
and its surroundings are old, proper
brick paving with joints will look more
in keeping.

Bricks and blocks coming right to the
edge of a pond will be especially
vulnerable to subsidence and therefore
need a good foundation.

Paving slabs Some of the worst pond
edges I have ever seen have been made
from slabs that could not be cut to cope
with curves. In one ugly instance, slabs
were laid in a curve up to the water's

edge so that the joints splayed out into
large wedges filled with mortar and
some pebbles.

Modest stepping in and out of the
slabs can work much better, but only if
the curved pond edge is modified to
accommodate this stepped effect.

There are obviously many types of
slabs which can be used. Rustic, imitation stone slabs laid to a random

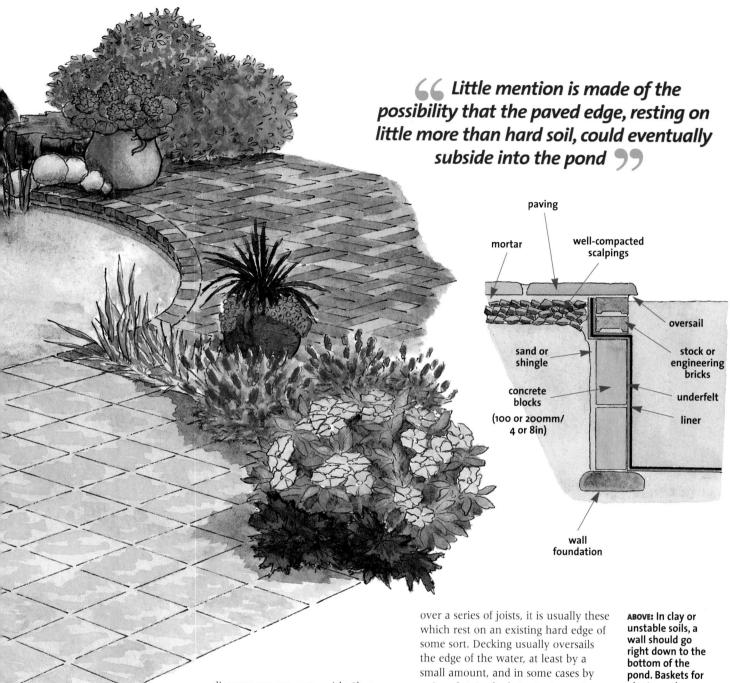

paving

mortar

well-compacted scalpings

oversail

sand or shingle

stock or engineering bricks

concrete blocks

underfelt

(100 or 200mm/ 4 or 8in)

liner

wall foundation

ABOVE: In clay or unstable soils, a wall should go right down to the bottom of the pond. Baskets for plants can be supported at various heights within the pond

pattern using a variety of sizes look good alongside an informal pool, while light-coloured textured slabs perhaps 45cm (18in) square can give a formal or straight-sided pool a more modern or possibly Mediterranean appearance.

If a curved edge is needed, slabs can be cut, but achieving a concave curve can be difficult because the disc cutter tends to bind on the sides of the cut. To minimise damage to the cutter when very thick slabs are involved, I suggest you use a belt-driven petrol machine together with the smallest

disc you can get away with. If you use an electric machine, take care not to strain the motor.

Just as with curves cut into brick or block paving, the cut slabs will need an edging of bricks or blocks.

Real stone Slabs of real stone can of course look very attractive, although they are often much thicker than manufactured slabs and therefore a little more difficult to lay. Real stone can also become especially slippery if laid in areas which are constantly in shade or beneath trees.

The most practical way of using real stone around curved edges is to pave with broken pieces as crazy paving, which can look attractive if the mortar joint widths are kept to a minimum.

Decking Since decking is usually laid

over a series of joists, it is usually these which rest on an existing hard edge of some sort. Decking usually oversails the edge of the water, at least by a small amount, and in some cases by quite a lot. In the latter instance, it may be cantilevered over the water and secured on land, but if it over-hangs the water by several feet, it may require supports down onto the floor of the pond for extra stability.

Safety can become an issue here since there is a much greater tendency for someone to fall off a suspended deck than from a normal paved edge, so some sort of safety rail could be needed.

It is also important never to use pressure-treated timber or poisonous preservatives over water, but instead to use untreated hardwoods – or non-toxic preservatives. Unlike any other form of paved edge, a deck may need stabilising since just sitting on a hard edge makes it vulnerable to sliding out of position.

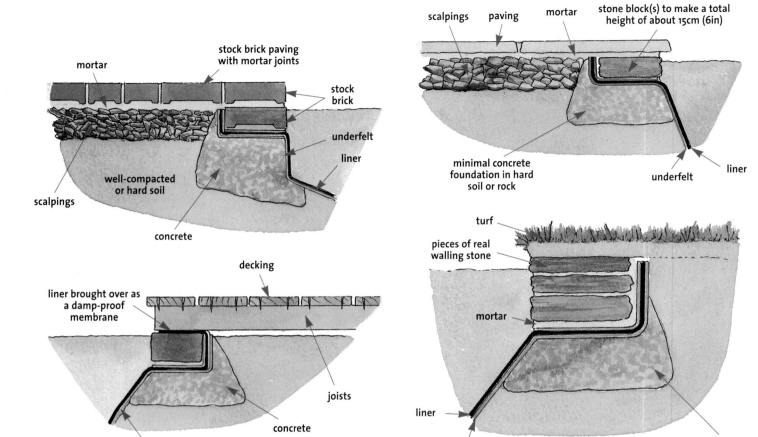

Hiding the liner

To conceal the liner and to provide a firm foundation, you will have to adopt a completely different approach from that normally described and illustrated.

If the paved edges are to remain stable, they must be set on a proper foundation.

Where the soil is quite hard, chalk for example, this might be just 15cm (6in) of concrete laid on a level and reasonably wide shelf cut in all around the pond about 30cm (12in) down from the top.

In soft soil or in clay this shelf must be cut much closer to the bottom of the pond or the base of the pond itself so that a wall can be built up to support the paving above. In this case the wall might be made from concrete blocks, stopping about 15cm (6in) below the proposed paving.

It will be easier to use half blocks or inexpensive bricks to build a curved wall. Once these 'foundations' are complete, a thick underfelt or geotextile matting must be laid over the whole excavation and out onto the top edges of the pool.

Then the liner is laid in exactly the same way, leaving the shapes of the foundations clearly visible underneath.

At this stage the pool is filled to just below the shelf so that the liner is properly settled. If this is not done now, water added later could pull on the liner and small walls build on top of it.

Depending upon the style of paving used, a low wall of either stone, bricks or perhaps blocks can be built up on

the shelf so that it finishes just beneath the proposed paving. You should work this distance out when setting the foundation.

Block paviors are not really designed for wall building since they often have bevelled corners, but in this case the wall is so small that this design point may not really matter.

Extra underfelt must be used under small walls and also anywhere else sharp edges or extra stress are likely to put strain on the liner. You can see from the diagrams that the liner comes up and passes behind the low wall.

As this is built, so thought should be given to an overflow. Without one, the pool will fill to just beneath the paving and in a storm it may briefly flood over the edges. A smallish pipe set into the wall and taken through the liner just below the paving will help to avoid flooding.

In clay soil any walls must be backfilled with sand or shingle to take up any soil movement.

The liner is trimmed off level with the top of the low wall. Once the pool has been filled to the top, the water level would have to drop at least 15cm (6in) before any of the liner became visible. In addition, it will be possible to stand right on the edge of any paving without any fear of subsidence.

Gorgeous gushers

How to install fountains and overcome some common problems

ABOVE: Ammonite fountain from Arcadian Garden Features Ltd

E ach year, perhaps more than ever before, all sorts of fountains are springing up in gardens all over Britain: large ones, little ones, bubbling stones, spitting lions and even squirting tortoises.

Some work very well and look fantastic, but others may stop working after a short while and look pretty awful. As with almost any garden feature, there are some simple rules to follow if a fountain is to be successful.

Not all that many years ago nearly all garden fountains were either simple patterned sprays of water emerging from a pool, a jet of water spurting from a small statue or water pouring from the mouth of a wall-mounted lion's head down into a small pool.

Now we have a choice ranging from fountains in the grand style which can be programmed to give a whole range of displays, to a variety of child-safe features where water

bubbles from the centre of a large boulder or millstone.

Water can be seen shooting from the mouth of a stone frog, lion's head or even a tortoise set into a border. Here the water seems to disappear into a pile of stones – but actually ends up back in an underground reservoir.

The distinction between what might be construed as a fountain or perhaps a cascade blurs when you see an old-fashioned 'well'

"A submersible pump can be damaged if it is not completely submerged in water"

"Get these the wrong way around and you have a millstone bursting into a massive geyser and a fountain producing a meaningless dribble"

MAKING A FOAMING GEYSER

If you cannot afford the necessary special nozzle – or you enjoy experimenting – try the following idea based on having some kind of elevated pool or reservoir within a main pool.

If the pipe rising vertically from a submersible pump comes right out of the water, then the obvious result is a plain jet of water, reminiscent of a burst water main. If, however, this same pipe ends just beneath the surface, say by 5-10mm (¼-⅜in), the water has to force its way through this thin layer before rising above the surface.

In the process it picks up air and emerges as a mixture of air and water – a foaming geyser in fact.

The effect can be adjusted by either changing the flow or the distance the pipe ends below the surface.

In an open pond this technique is too unreliable since the water level can vary and, perhaps, even fall below the top of the pipe. If, however, the idea is built into an 'inner' pool or vessel, then once the initial burst of water has topped it up to overflowing, the depth and effect will remain constant. When the pump is eventually turned off, water in this 'inner' pool will drop to the rim of the pipe, resulting in another initial but short-lived jet of water when the pump is next turned on.

All this can be produced on a large and dramatic scale using a powerful pump in the main pool or on a small scale using an urn or half-barrel suspended on a grille over a hidden reservoir. Where a pool has been designed to attract wildlife, especially amphibians, it is better not to have a vigorous fountain or anything which disturbs the surface of the water too violently.

ABOVE: Island of foam produced with an inner pool – see cross section

pump constantly pouring water, or water cascading down through an arrangement of dainty copper or bronze cups.

In many cases, sound is as important as the visual effect. There is little doubt that the sound of moving water can seem to have a cooling effect on a hot patio, but I do wonder about claims that it can mask the sound of traffic from a busy nearby road.

Lighting, too, can work its magic and bring water alive at night. As a general rule, a small water feature should be near a seating area or close to the house where its detail can be appreciated from close quarters.

Larger and more dramatic fountains can make an impressive focal point in a garden and should, therefore, be viewed from a greater distance away.

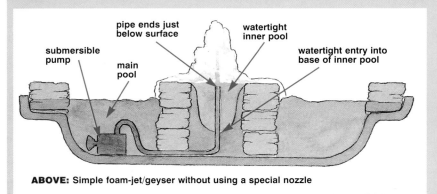

pipe ends just below surface
watertight inner pool
submersible pump
main pool
watertight entry into base of inner pool

ABOVE: Simple foam-jet/geyser without using a special nozzle

Clean water

Most fountains need to run on clean water if they are to perform reliably. Where a conventional spray fountain is being used in a pond, the pond water may have to be filtered by a special unit.

Where pond life is not wanted, additives like chlorine or algaecides can be added, but chlorine must be used at the correct concentration if it is not to smell, or harm pets which might drink the water. Additives can be especially useful in many other types of 'lifeless' fountains.

The pumps used in conjunction with a filtration unit take in both water and dirt – they do not have their own filter. A fountain pump, on the other hand, does have its own filter to protect nozzles from becoming blocked, so where a pond is to be filtered and have a fountain, it is usual to use two pumps – one for each function.

A large spray fountain will obviously need a much more powerful pump than a bubbling millstone – get these the wrong way around and you have a millstone bursting into a massive geyser and a fountain producing a meaningless dribble.

ABOVE: Drilled stone provides attractive effect

Fountain types

Apart from lion's heads and conventional spray fountains, there are geyser 'foam' jets, *also see panel*. These are designed to suck in air and mix it with the water to produce a lively column of foaming water which, with an appropriate pump and nozzle, can reach a height of a metre or more.

The 'bell' jet compresses a flow of water and deflects it downwards to produce a glassy mushroom of water.

Lighting can have dramatic

"There is little doubt that the sound of moving water can seem to have a cooling effect on a hot patio but I do wonder about claims that it can mask the sound of traffic"

results here, but dirty water could soon spoil the effect – the water must be free from debris.

Solar-powered pumps are now available. Their output is not very substantial but this technology does make it possible to have a modest fountain where it was previously out of the question.

LION'S HEAD

A wall-mounted lion's head is usually cast into a block, made from either concrete or reconstituted stone. It would therefore be built into a wall.

A small pipe feeds water through from the back into the mouth, so these features are best built into a backing wall from the outset.

If they are added somehow into an existing wall there is always the question of how to hide the delivery pipe.

On something like your own garage wall or some other free-standing wall within the garden, it is easier to run the pipe behind rather than 'chase out' a

channel down the front face.

The lion's head pours water either directly into a pool below or into a small suspended vessel/shell which then, in turn, overflows into the main pool.

Much smaller features – combination wall 'masks' – are available which pour water directly into their own small reservoir. This is all part of the same casting, so that the whole thing can be hung on a wall. A tiny pump circulates the water, but there is always a danger that such a small reservoir might soon run dry in hot weather.

Because it is self-contained, there is no plumbing as such, but a special power supply is still needed.

In the case of the larger lion's head and the separate pool, a pump is situated in the pool. The delivery pipe will be briefly visible as it leaves the pool and enters the wall, but can often be hidden with a potted aquatic plant.

BELOW: Don't fancy a toad? This beast is operated on the same principle

ABOVE: Self-contained lion's head feature with its own pump in a small reservoir of water. The reservoir must never be allowed to run dry. The feature requires a suitable electricity supply

RIGHT: Fountains can be very grand, like this dolphin creation at Harewood House…

LEFT:… or very simple, like these pots

CHRIS SKARBON

Common problems

Lion's head dribbles This may be due to poor mouth design or to an inadequate flow of water. A better flow can often overcome this – so long as the jet of water does not then miss the reservoir.

Water is blown back This can result in a serious water loss over a period of a few days because the wall is likely to absorb the water rather than return it to the pool. An existing wall could be sprayed with colourless silicone or painted with a colourless resin. There is then a good chance that water would run off and into the pool. Here is a good case for building the wall and the pool as one from the outset.

Jet of water is too vigorous A flow valve can often be fitted on the outflow pipe right next to the pump and adjusted accordingly. It is often, in fact, better to use a pump which is initially too powerful, along with a flow valve so that the flow may be increased after a period of time if the pump loses its efficiency.

BUBBLING STONES, MILLSTONES ETC.

In most cases these are suspended by means of a strong steel grid – along with pebbles and small boulders – over an underground tank of water.

Kits are available in most large garden centres. They include a small plastic reservoir together with a plastic cover. This cover can support a bed of stones – not large boulders – and has a central hole for a fountain on the submersible pump below. Unfortunately, the reservoir is very small and may run low on water in hot weather.

Common problems

Reservoir and pump running dry A submersible pump can be damaged if it is not completely submerged in water, and unfortunately this type of water feature can easily run low without you realising it. A good-sized reservoir will help even though it may be more difficult to set up initially. Another idea is to fix a narrow rigid tube

between the stones and down onto the bottom of the reservoir, then to make a dipstick out of a split cane and use this down the tube to check the depth of water. I have also seen a simple 'float' used in the tube, calibrated to show the depth of water. All these arrangements must be installed discreetly.

Excessive water loss Since some water is inevitably lost through evaporation, the best way to assess whether there is an additional problem is to run the fountain on a dull drizzly day when the humidity is obviously very high. Normally water loss on these days is negligible. The most common reason for

"Lighting can work its magic and bring water alive at night"

excessive water loss is due to a fountain which is too vigorous for the space it is in. On windy days especially, water can easily splash outside the catchment area of the reservoir and be lost. Apart from reducing the intensity of the fountain, it may be possible to create a plastic or butyl apron around the reservoir in such a way as to catch and drain all this water back to where it belongs.

RIGHT: Spitting toad can be placed in a border and arranged to project its water into a concealed underground reservoir

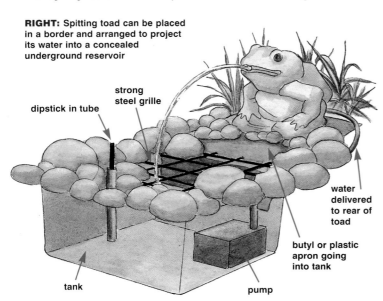

dipstick in tube

strong steel grille

water delivered to rear of toad

butyl or plastic apron going into tank

tank

pump

MAINTENANCE AND SAFETY

Pumps need cleaning and servicing from time to time so they must be easily accessible. This may not be easy to achieve if there is a bed of heavy boulders lying over the top.

Never drag a pump out by its electric cable. Many pumps are very simple and not complicated to dismantle and clean once they have been disconnected from the electricity supply.

Installation must be carried out by a qualified electrician. Power will most likely be delivered to the 'poolside' by an armoured cable to special exterior, all-weather sockets. The power is usually taken from a suitably fused spur within the house and protected by a circuit breaker. It is always worth having several exterior sockets fitted so that lighting and maybe a filter can be added.

That's how accidents happen – small children and ponds can be a lethal mixture

Taking precautions

There are many things you can do to make your pond safer for visitors and unattractive to herons and cats

If a pond is large enough for fish then it is probably large enough for children to fall into.

A sizeable pool, of course, is likely to attract a host of other creatures which need an environment offering protection from the unwelcome attentions of herons and cats.

Safety in all sorts of ways is, therefore, an important consideration in the water garden.

Protecting people

Although you might have waited patiently for your own children to have grown up before putting a large fish pond in the garden, it could seem no time at all before little grand-children are running around and making you think of ways to make the pond safe – at least on a temporary basis.

One of the most effective safety barriers is a picket fence. It can be both attractive and robust, but must be at least 75cm (2ft 6in) high. It need not be a permanent feature, since it can be slotted into sockets set flush with the ground – possibly square-section plastic rain-water piping which is about 65mm (2¹/₂in) across.

With one end made slightly smaller, wooden posts 75mm (3in) square can be used as uprights which are slotted in and out. The fence itself must be in manageable lengths, say 1.2m (4ft), and fixed together in a way which will make setting up and dismantling quick and easy.

The sockets must be blocked off when not in use to prevent them from filling with rubbish. This could be done with flush, loose-fitting blocks of wood with an 'eye' set down into the top so that they can be lifted out with a hook.

Wood swells when it is wet so all the posts and blocks must be an easy fit.

Metal hoop fencing, similar to that used around parks and school playgrounds, is another possibility which, if painted olive green, will 'disappear' into a background of greenery.

It could be that the metal fencing would be best as a permanent barrier around the back of the pond while removable picket fencing is used in front – this arrangement of fencing should also keep most dogs out of the pond.

Visitors who use wheelchairs would probably feel vulnerable if paved edges had no means of preventing the chair from slipping into the water.

Ideally, a suitable barrier

Temporary picket fencing, set into sock-
ets, is designed to prevent young children from falling
into the pool along its most vulnerable side. At a height of about 75cm
(2ft 6in) it will also deter herons. Around the other sides of the pond are horizontal wires – against herons – and some
metal hoop fencing – all green so as to appear as invisible as possible. The wires coincide with an area of herbaceous planting
which in winter and spring will be almost non-existent, leaving the pond pictured very exposed to herons. Nearside planting is
taller and shrubby, making this area less attractive for herons

should be included at the planning stage – it might be difficult
to install one once the paving
has been laid.

Most barriers are made from
square-section or tubular steel.
A horizontal bar about 215mm
(9in) above the ground is weld-
ed to strong and reasonably frequent uprights and is more likely to be permanent than removable although it will only be
needed alongside access points
around the pond.

Herons

Herons are considered Public
Enemy Number One by most fish
owners. It is important to under-
stand a little about their habits if
they are to be kept at bay.

Apart from fish, herons also
eat small mammals, reptiles,
insects, worms and even small
birds – all of which you may
have encouraged, on purpose,

"Very large ponds tend to attract ducks, moorhens and coots which often sleep around the edges at night, making them easy pickings for foxes"

by creating shallow areas around
the edges of the pond.

Herons feed mostly at dawn
and dusk. Ponds with steep sides
and a dense covering of lily pads
make life difficult for a heron
which prefers shallow banks and
water, and needs to see the fish it
is about to catch.

Herons do like an open aspect
which gives them a good view of
approaching danger, so a pond
well shrouded in shrubs and tall
undergrowth is less likely to be
attacked. A heron – like us –
would find it very difficult to see
fish through a rippling surface, so
anything – like a spray of water –
which disrupts the surface is likely to provide some protection.

Other devices

Porsof artificial lily pads are
green and made from a plastic
which floats. They are easy to
cut, overlap and arrange to form
a dense barrier – mainly around
the edges of the pond where
fish are most at danger.

Real waterlily pads may not
always grow right around the
edges and will be less evident in
winter.

Netting can be stretched
across the pond, just above the
surface. The mesh, however,
must be no wider that 5cm
(2in) knot-to-knot and it should
be reasonably robust so that it
does not sag too much and, ideally, should be green in colour.

Horizontal wires stretched
around the pond edges must be
at least 75cm (2ft 6in) above the
ground and right at the water's
edge so that the heron cannot
stand on the inside.

These wires have to be a permanent fixture and may be
rather obvious. They could be
green and need not be especially
thick, so long as the vertical –
often metal – supports are
robust.

A heron will find it difficult
to take fish from a pond where
the sides are almost vertical and
the water is at least 60cm (2ft)
below ground level. Effective
though this might be, small
mammals could fall in and

The picket fence has been removed but this open section remains protected by an infrared sensor and an alarm. The rest of the fencing can stay in place since it does not spoil the view of the pond

drown unless some netting is draped over the edges to help them climb out.

The Scarey Man Fall-Guy, available from Clarratts Ltd, is an inflatable scarecrow which suddenly inflates and rises up from a control box every 15 minutes or so before deflating after 20 seconds.

It is powered by a rechargeable 12V battery and can be programmed to appear day and/or night. It lights up at night and has a switchable siren.

Wingaway Bird Scarers play digitally recorded bird alarm cries at random intervals day or night. Various models are available, along with a selection of bird cries, including the heron's.

The devices can be powered by batteries or from the mains via an AC adapter. The type of bird cry is selected by turning a dial.

PondGard Heron/Cat Scare is

a device which, when triggered by a tensioned trip wire, produces a loud crack from an exploding cap.

The height of the trip wire can be varied but has to be permanently stretched across all the access points.

It is, therefore, slightly vulnerable to accidental damage and, if broken, the wire can be quite difficult to repair and re-tension.

Cypri-Gard is an infrared sensor which detects the arrival of an intruder and triggers a well-aimed jet of water. It has to be connected to a garden hose and is powered by batteries.

Although highly effective, it can, of course, catch humans unawares! Similar products work on the same principle, but utter various high-frequency noises instead of squirting water. The pitch can usually be

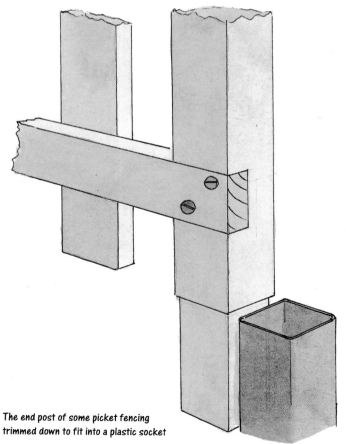

The end post of some picket fencing trimmed down to fit into a plastic socket

A wooden block and steel eye to slot loosely into the ground sockets

varied to frighten different creatures, such as cats.

Waterfowl

Very large ponds tend to attract ducks, moorhens and coots which often sleep around the edges at night, making them easy pickings for foxes.

An island in the centre of the ponds will usually offer ducks a reasonable degree of safety and might be used as a nest site as well as for sleeping.

It may be difficult to build up a solid island from the floor of an established pond but a floating platform could be equally successful, anchored securely right in the centre.

Structural safety

In spite of today's warmer climate, there are still many areas in the UK where ponds freeze over in winter.

Ponds made from moulded plastic or fibreglass, some ponds made from concrete, and especially those which are raised above ground, may be damaged by freezing and thawing.

Floating pieces of wood around the edges, floating balls or even installing a pool heater, can all help to relieve pressure and, therefore, help to prevent structural damage. Relieving the pressure may also be helpful for the fish.

Pond electrics

The only way to ensure that pond electrics are installed safely is to use a fully qualified electrician. Even if the electrics are fixed up on a DIY basis they should still be checked over by an electrician before the power is switched on.

Armoured cable is likely to bring power from the house to the poolside. Its connection to the mains supply will almost certainly include an appropriately fused spur and an earth safety trip.

At the poolside 'all weather' or waterproof sockets must be arranged to take whatever appliances are required. These could include a pump, filter, pool heater, lighting and so on.

Any cable carrying the full 240V to an appliance must be protected, perhaps in conduit.

Poor electrical installation and water can become a lethal combination.

Weather protection

Some of the more exotic and sophisticated fish, koi included, may suffer if the water temperature drops too low or fluctuates excessively during the winter and early spring.

Covers made from rigid or semi-rigid plastic fixed to frames can help to minimise this although it is important to leave some air gaps.

Heavy downpours of rain can cause flash flooding and a surge of water to leave the pool via the overflow. If the overflow pipe has a diameter of about 25mm (1in) or more, it is possible for fish to be washed out of the pond.

A filter or some netting will prevent this from happening, although it must never be allowed to become clogged.

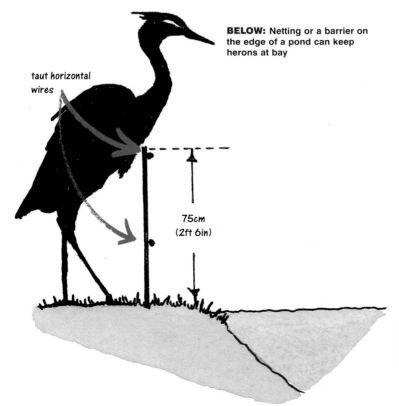

taut horizontal wires

BELOW: Netting or a barrier on the edge of a pond can keep herons at bay

75cm (2ft 6in)

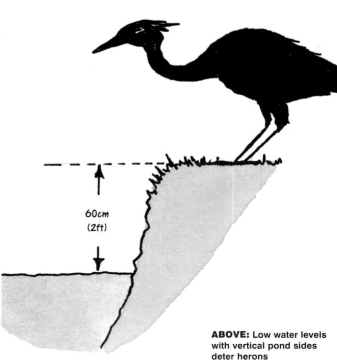

60cm (2ft)

ABOVE: Low water levels with vertical pond sides deter herons

BOG GARDENS

Arum lily
(*Zantedeschia
aethiopica*) is one
of the classic bog-
garden plants

Small but boggily formed

Three lovely bog areas for the tiniest of gardens

Mini bog on a slope

A mini bog garden can even be positioned in a small, sloping garden. As you can see in the drawing, a hole has been dug into the slope and a supporting wall built from logs or poles in order to create a level area. This has then been lined with butyl, fitted with a dip stick assembly and filled with soil. The liner comes up a little way into the slope behind the excavation, so that when soil is added, this particular area will remain drier than the rest. There is also a small, butyl-lined pocket in front of the log wall for some extra planting, but this is likely to dry out from time to time, so less dependent bog plants must go in here. Plants included in this bed – which measures about 1m (3ft) wide and 1.2m (3ft 6) long – are:

1 *Eriophorum angustifolium* (cotton grass)

2 *Mentha aquatica* (water mint)

3 *Mimulus luteus* (monkey flower)

4 *Acorus gramineus* 'Variegata' (a striped rush)

5 *Viola palustris* (bog violet)

6 *Drosera rotundifolia* (sundew)

7 *Myosotis palustris* (water forget-me-not)

In the front *Primula vulgaris*, *Primula denticulata* and *Viola labradorica* grow in moist garden soil.

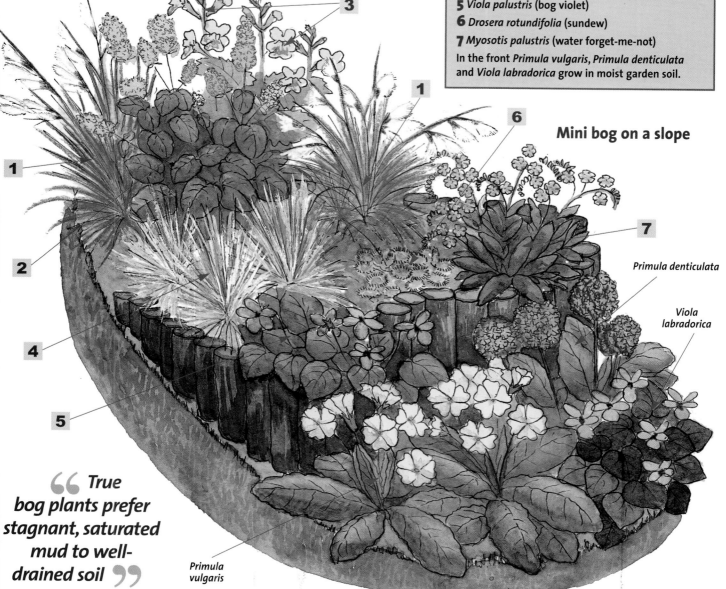

Mini bog on a slope

Primula denticulata

Viola labradorica

Primula vulgaris

> ❝ **True bog plants prefer stagnant, saturated mud to well-drained soil** ❞

Mini bog in a half barrel

Here, a half barrel measuring about 75cm (2ft 3) across has been set part way into the ground. It may not need a liner since barrels are usually watertight. It should, however, be given some drain holes a few centimetres down from the top so that the top zone of soil can remain less wet than the rest. A dip-stick assembly will also be very useful. Most barrels are made from oak and therefore need no wood preservative, but the steel bands will need rust proofing with a suitable paint. Plants included here are:

1 *Lobelia cardinalis* 'Queen Victoria'
2 *Iris kaempferi* 'Higo'
3 *Hosta* 'Groundmaster' or similar
4 *Hosta* 'Halcyon'
5 *Polystichum polyblephrum* (a relatively small fern)
6 *Lysimachia nummularia* 'Aurea' (this also thrives in dry soil)

In front of the bog, in normal garden soil, are *Ophiopogon planiscapus* 'Nigrescens' (a black grass), *Stachys lanata* 'Silver Carpet' (a non-flowering strain) and *Houttuynia cordata* 'Chameleon'

There are many beautiful plants, both wild and cultivated, which require constant moisture if they are to flourish. In nature, the only place they are likely to survive is in soil which is always wet – a bog in other words.

However, many of these bog – or marginal – plants will survive in ordinary garden soil providing it is kept moist. Some will even tolerate dry conditions for a limited period and end up growing – not always happily – alongside many other border flowers before eventually dying out after a prolonged dry spell.

Creating a bog garden is easy. The results can be very rewarding and often quite spectacular, with many of the bog plants growing to immense proportions.

Mini bog in a half barrel

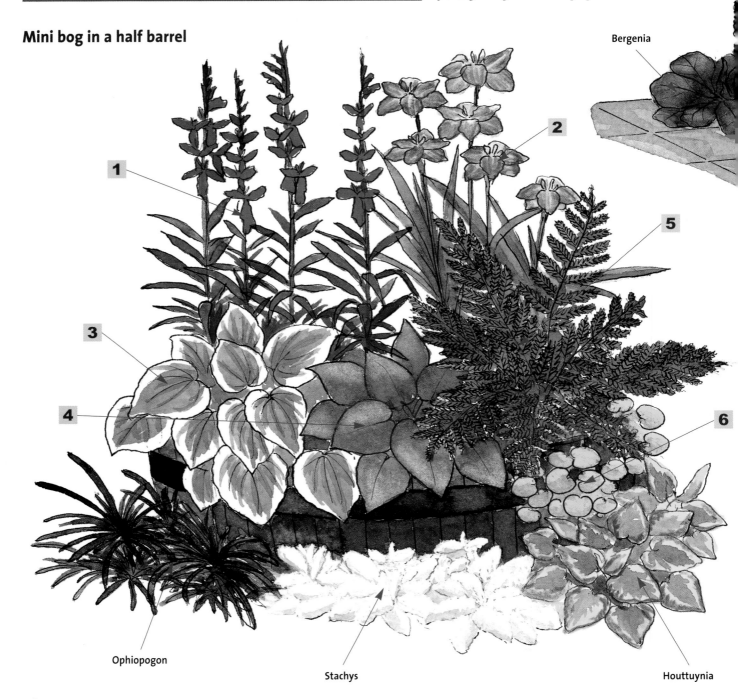

Bergenia

Ophiopogon

Stachys

Houttuynia

Rocky bog

Lamium

Arabis

Festuca

This implies that a bog garden should be quite extensive to accommodate all this growth, but what if your garden is very small? It will not be possible to grow many of the largest bog plants, so choice will have to be restricted to the relatively small ones which would then make it possible to enjoy a tiny bog garden. There are three quite different ideas shown here. Outwardly they look dissimilar, but internally their construction is very similar.

What to aim for

True bog plants prefer stagnant, saturated mud to well-drained soil so you will need to create an area which will flood almost to the surface.

Ideally, the top few centimetres should, however, be drier than the rest so that any plants which prefer damp rather than saturated soil can keep their roots in this zone.

In a large bog garden, drier areas can be achieved by having some parts higher than others, but in a tiny bog

garden a drain hole a few centimetres down from the top may be the only way to achieve this.

Drainage

There is some value in having an area right in the bottom of the bog which is free from soil and is just stones and water. In each of the three examples illustrated, a butyl liner together with an underfelt has been used, although in practice the wooden tub may not need lining. There is a layer of stones or lump charcoal about 75mm (3in) deep in the bottom of each structure, with a piece of geotextile matting over the top to prevent soil from washing down and blocking up the space between the stones.

Soil

Soil should be a good-quality medium, weed-free loam with plenty of well-rotted manure or humus mixed in and a pH of less than 6.5 – acid. It should be well compacted so that it does not sink too much after planting, and nowhere

Rocky bog

This bog area has been built on top of the ground. It might perhaps go on a patio against a fence in which case the rear supporting wall could be in concrete blocks which would take up less space and cost less than rocks. Ideally, rocks should be built up to a height of at least 30cm (12in). This particular example is about 1.8m (6ft) long and 1.2m (4ft) wide/deep. It is lined with butyl but in order to ensure there is a slightly drier zone near the top, the butyl could be stopped a few centimetres down from the top edges. A dip-stick assembly would be especially useful here because the bog area is not very deep and may therefore dry out quickly in hot sunny weather. If the feature is built against a fence, then quite tall plants could be included, but only if they do not take up too much lateral space. Plants that have been used here are:

1 *Astilbe* 'Elizabeth Bloom' (or similar)

2 *Glyceria spectabilis* (a spectacular golden grass)

3 *Rodgersia pinnata* 'Elegans' (its foliage resembles that of the horse chestnut)

4 *Houttuynia cordata* 'Flore Pleno' (double white flowers and dark green leaves)

5 *Lamium maculatum* 'White Nancy'

6 *Ajuga reptans* 'Braunherz'

These last two will also grow quite happily in ordinary garden soil.

In front of the bog area – assuming there are soil pockets available, and there might be on a patio, for instance – are *Bergenia cordifolia*, *Festuca glauca* (blue grass), *Arabis ferdinandi-coburgii* 'Variegata' and more lamium.

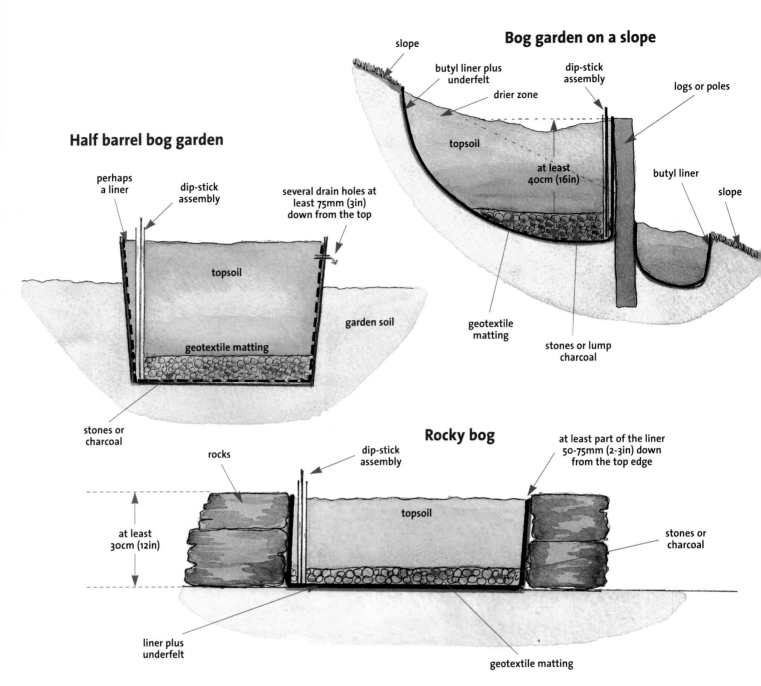

Half barrel bog garden

perhaps a liner

dip-stick assembly

several drain holes at least 75mm (3in) down from the top

topsoil

garden soil

geotextile matting

stones or charcoal

Bog garden on a slope

slope

butyl liner plus underfelt

drier zone

dip-stick assembly

logs or poles

topsoil

at least 40cm (16in)

butyl liner

slope

geotextile matting

stones or lump charcoal

Rocky bog

rocks

dip-stick assembly

at least part of the liner 50-75mm (2-3in) down from the top edge

topsoil

at least 30cm (12in)

stones or charcoal

liner plus underfelt

geotextile matting

should this soil come into contact with the surrounding garden, otherwise valuable moisture could be drawn out of the bog into the ground around. Bringing the butyl liner just out of the soil can help to act as a damp-proof membrane and prevent this leaching.

Water gauge

Once the bog garden has been filled and planted it will be difficult to tell how moist it is apart from testing with

your finger. A narrow rigid tube can be set down into the stones, before the soil is added, and brought a few centimetres up above the final soil level. A thin stick, painted matt black, can then be lowered into this tube to gauge where the water level is – in the same way as you might check the level of engine oil in your car.

Position

Bog gardens succeed in sun or shade although they are unlikely to thrive deep under the canopy of a large dark tree. Although only relatively small bog garden plants are being used here, some could still reach a height of 60cm (24in) or so and this might have to be taken into account when deciding exactly where the mini bog should be positioned in relation to the surrounding plants and garden.

Care

It is important to remember that most bog plants are perennials and therefore die back in winter. During the summer, their growth and colour can be enhanced by feeding with liquid fertilisers every few weeks, especially since the plants will, in effect, be growing in a large container and could eventually run out of nutrients if not fed.

Do not be tempted to make holes in the liner near the base of the bog, otherwise water will drain out and be drawn out by the surrounding garden. Similarly, do not allow garden soil to come over the edge of the bog area and touch the boggy soil otherwise, once again, moisture will be sucked out. The bog must be kept isolated from the rest of the garden if moisture levels are to be maintained.

> **Once the bog garden has been filled and planted it will be difficult to tell how moist it is apart from testing with your finger**

RIGHT: Flowers and foliage make a fabulous bog garden. Here we see candelabra primulas, the purple leaves of *Rodgersia podophylla* 'Rotlaub' and the white plumes of *Aruncus sylvester* (goat's beard)

**A well-designed bog garden provides a wide range of conditions for a huge variety of plants.
Here are some sound guidelines for making one**

Bog garden beginnings

Some plants need constant moisture in the soil – and 'bog plants' are the best! They will die if the soil in which they are growing dries out for any length of time, and are nearly all herbaceous perennials, providing interest from February through to summer's end.

While some bog plants grow happily in ordinary garden soil so long as there is some shade and the ground seldom dries out completely, others thrive only in constant dampness or even standing water.

With many plants falling between these extremes, a well-designed bog garden should provide all these conditions, so that choice is not limited by the degree of moisture.

Position

Some shade is better than none, although the area immediately beneath a low tree canopy is far from ideal due to falling leaves and seeds, very poor light and tree roots hindering excavation.

Although the project is contained within a liner, the bog garden should not be totally immersed in weed-infested soil.

As an 'island' feature within a large expanse of lawn, or as an extension to a pond, a bog garden can be particularly effective. It can be placed next to a pond so as to appear part of it, but must be physically separated.

This is because the high evaporation rate of a bog garden could result in a pond being robbed of too much moisture. Only where there is a large pond, with a constant, natural input of water, can the bog garden be successfully integrated.

It works best in a flat piece of land or on a plateau rather than on a slope, although a sloping garden could have a level terraced section created for the purpose.

Position must also have a bearing on bog garden plants' high susceptibility to rabbit, deer and slug damage; also, to avoid the effects of high winds, cold winds or salt spray, choose a sheltered, lightly shaded place which is not in a frost hollow.

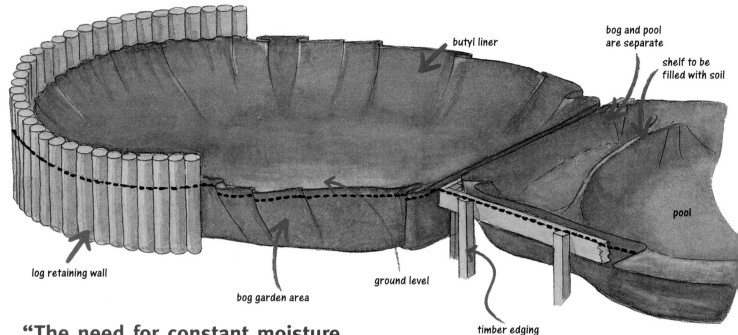

bog and pool
are separate

shelf to be
filled with soil

butyl liner

pool

log retaining wall

bog garden area

ground level

timber edging

"The need for constant moisture dictates that bog garden soil must be kept separate from that of the surrounding garden"

ABOVE: The cool greens of hostas – this is *H. fortunei* 'Marginata Alba' – go well with the hot candelabra primulas

ABOVE: Constructing a bog garden next to a pond – the dotted line denotes ground level. Part of the bog garden is to be slightly raised, and the timber retaining wall protrudes by about 40cm (16in) above ground. Timber shuttering on the pool edge helps support a butyl liner. The bog garden has a separate liner, and is treated separately from the pool. On completion they will appear joined

Design

The need for constant moisture dictates that bog garden soil must be kept separate from that of the surrounding garden. This is achieved by lining the excavation with a watertight liner, *see below.*

The excavation should be about 45cm (18in) deep on average, with fairly steep sides. To provide conditions ranging from almost constant wetness to relatively dry but always damp areas, the dug out – or new – soil goes back, profiled so that some areas are below the flood level and others built up above it.

Many bog plants grow large, so the bigger your bog garden the better as a small one will restrict plant choice.

Appearance may be partly dictated by the size and shape of an adjacent pool, but a bog garden built in isolation can take any shape.

It could start as a broadly oval, slightly mounded area, narrowing to become a mock stream or ditch which becomes progressively wet as it meanders its way across the lawn, possibly with a bridge; or it could be small, suggestive of an oasis, with the wettest section across the centre.

It is, however, always important to have the fullest range of profiles that your space allows.

Liner

Butyl, which is the material least likely to deteriorate with age and the hardest to damage or puncture, is the best – and often most expensive – liner choice. Less dear is a 500-gauge or more PVC liner, but this is more prone to damage.

All liners should be sandwiched between a geotextile underfelt which protects against sharp objects.

To work out the size to buy, follow this formula:
overall length = bog garden length + twice its maximum depth + about 30cm (12in); overall width = bog garden width + twice its maximum depth + about 30cm (12in). The under/overfelt should be of similar size.

Backfilling

Providing the excavated soil is free from perennial weeds and is all fertile topsoil, then it could be reused.

A heavy loam with plenty of added humus or well-rotted

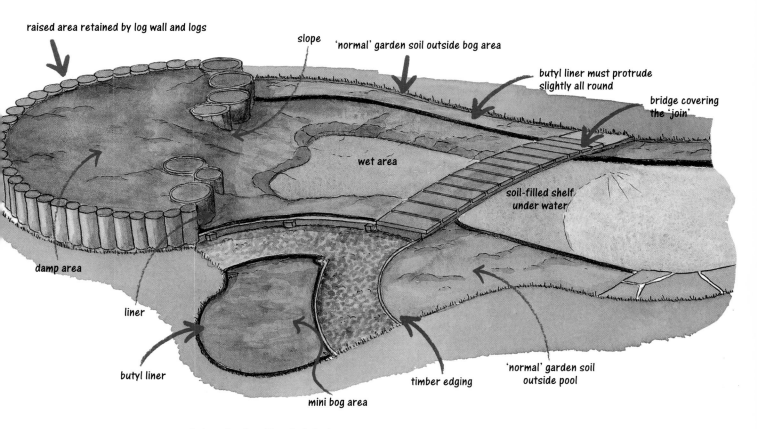

raised area retained by log wall and logs

slope

'normal' garden soil outside bog area

butyl liner must protrude slightly all round

bridge covering the 'join'

wet area

soil-filled shelf under water

damp area

liner

butyl liner

mini bog area

timber edging

'normal' garden soil outside pool

ABOVE: The bog garden at Wakehurst Place in Sussex is looking good here

compost/manure with a pH of around 6.5 is ideal.

Charcoal can help prevent the soil from becoming too sour under the stagnant conditions which can prevail in a bog garden, although many true bog plants do not mind this.

So first spread a 15cm (6in) layer of lump charcoal over the bottom of the lined excavation, followed by another layer of matting.

Arrange the proportion of higher, dryer areas to the lower, wetter ones to suit your selection of plants – an average of two-thirds 'dry' to one-third 'very wet' tends to suit most circumstances.

The soil is replaced, compacted and profiled accordingly, with the wettest areas remaining

below the flood level of the liner.

At no point should bog garden soil come into contact with soil outside it. To prevent this from happening, the liner is brought to the surface vertically and trimmed so that about 1cm ($\frac{1}{2}$in) protrudes vertically from the soil.

This damp-proof barrier will soon be obscured by planting or lawn.

Where the bog garden is constructed next to a pool, it may be possible to continue the very wet area on the other side of the liner and into the adjacent pool edges, using soil-filled shelves or planting baskets just beneath the surface.

Plants growing under these conditions are termed 'marginals', and are at the extreme end of the bog-plant spectrum.

Mini-bog garden

Readers lacking the space to accommodate a full-sized bog garden can still build a small area for a few plants, but because keeping plants healthy in a restricted area of boggy soil can be more difficult, the construction is slightly different.

First, a hole not less that 90cm (3ft) across by 40cm (16in) is lined as before, again including the charcoal layer. The liner is brought up just above the soil surface, as before, but this time a series of small holes is made in the liner, about 10cm (4in) down from the top.

This action lowers the poten-

ABOVE: The excavation is back-filled with suitable soil so that one area is below flood level and the rest raised above it. A shelf adjacent to the pool is also back-filled with soil, most of which remains under the water. The bridge hides the point where bog and pool meet, and a gravel path to the bridge splits to pass either side of an isolated mini-bog area. Logs act as partial terracing

tial flood level and encourages limited contact with the surrounding garden soil, so that the mini-bog is less likely to be excessively wet.

Use of a dip stick allows moisture levels to be assessed. Before the soil is added, carefully insert into the charcoal layer

a rigid plastic 25mm (1in) diameter tube, long enough to rise above the finished soil level. A stick, sprayed matt black, can then be kept in the tube and used as a moisture-measuring device to let you know if more water should be added – before the plants wilt.

ABOVE: The larger bog garden can incorporate *Gunnera manicata*, seen here towards the bank, right

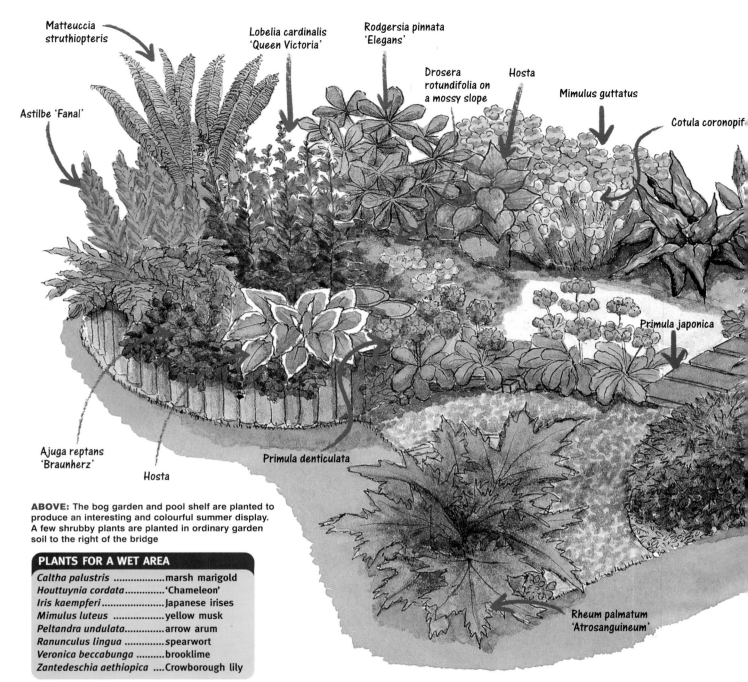

Matteuccia
struthiopteris

Lobelia cardinalis
'Queen Victoria'

Rodgersia pinnata
'Elegans'

Drosera
rotundifolia on
a mossy slope

Hosta

Mimulus guttatus

Cotula coronopif

Astilbe 'Fanal'

Primula japonica

Ajuga reptans
'Braunherz'

Hosta

Primula denticulata

Rheum palmatum
'Atrosanguineum'

ABOVE: The bog garden and pool shelf are planted to produce an interesting and colourful summer display. A few shrubby plants are planted in ordinary garden soil to the right of the bridge

PLANTS FOR A WET AREA

Caltha palustris	marsh marigold
Houttuynia cordata	'Chameleon'
Iris kaempferi	Japanese irises
Mimulus luteus	yellow musk
Peltandra undulata	arrow arum
Ranunculus lingua	spearwort
Veronica beccabunga	brooklime
Zantedeschia aethiopica	Crowborough lily

"Charcoal can help prevent the soil from becoming too sour under stagnant conditions"

ABOVE: Small formal bog garden containing pink *Astilbe* x *arendsii* 'Bressingham Beauty', with white *Iris laevigata* 'Snowdrift' in the foreground

Selecting, arranging

The range of plants is huge, in size going from the massive, rhubarb-like *Gunnera manicata* down to the insectivorous sundew Drosera, and it is important to know the potential size and shape of each plant.

Gunnera and other very large plants, like skunk cabbage *Lysichitum americanum*, are best reserved for the boggy edges of a large pond or lake, but the smaller 'ornamental rhubarb', *Rheum palmatum*, is suitable for smaller gardens.

A mini bog is useful to contain larger, more spreading plants; indeed, arranging shapes and sizes is more important than colour coordination.

The tiny sundew needs a mossy yet open area, with no over-shadowing from other plants, on the edge of the wettest part of the bog.

Astilbes, which develop tall, coloured plumes of flowers in early summer, will not want to be pressed up against spreaders like rheum.

Hostas and primulas grow happily in the same area, perhaps with some creeping plants between them, and small ferns should be happy under the canopy of spreading plants.

Maintenance

For the first year or so, picking out weeds and occasionally applying a foliar feed should be the only action necessary.

Applying fertilisers to the soil is generally inadvisable, but organic fertilisers – like seaweed products – are less likely to cause long-term problems, and

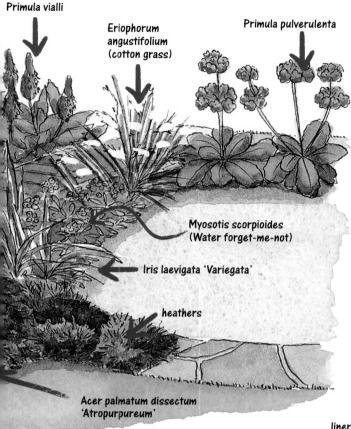

Primula vialli

Eriophorum
angustifolium
(cotton grass)

Primula pulverulenta

Myosotis scorpioides
(Water forget-me-not)

Iris laevigata 'Variegata'

heathers

Acer palmatum dissectum
'Atropurpureum'

The beautiful bog border at Beth Chatto's garden in Colchester, Essex

foliar feeding even less so.

After a year or two, some plants will have to be reduced by carefully digging them out, separating some of the newest crowns and replanting only these. Generally speaking, the procedure is as for plants in a herbaceous border. If using a fork, take pains not to damage the liner.

Some bog plants, like Lysichitum and Zantedeschia, are sensitive to frost, so will need some winter protection. Others may suffer pest damage, particularly from slugs, so require a non-toxic form of pest control.

The bog area may become home to frogs, toads, lizards, insects and even snakes, so all chemicals must be kept to the minimum.

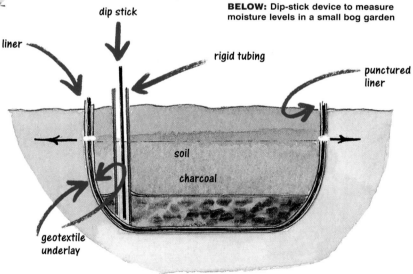

BELOW: Dip-stick device to measure moisture levels in a small bog garden

dip stick

liner

rigid tubing

punctured liner

soil

charcoal

geotextile underlay

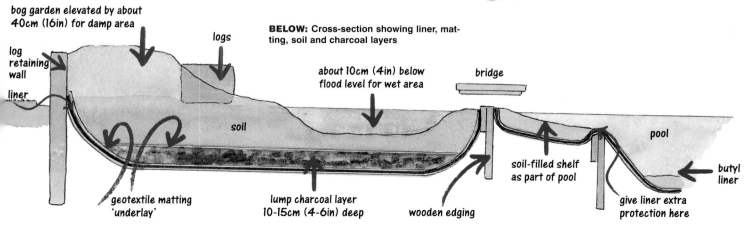

BELOW: Cross-section showing liner, matting, soil and charcoal layers

bog garden elevated by about 40cm (16in) for damp area

logs

log retaining wall

liner

about 10cm (4in) below flood level for wet area

bridge

soil

pool

soil-filled shelf as part of pool

butyl liner

geotextile matting 'underlay'

lump charcoal layer 10-15cm (4-6in) deep

wooden edging

give liner extra protection here

A tranquil scene at Isabella Plantation,
Richmond Park, Surrey

FORMAL OR WILD?

Weighing up the merits of
two very different approaches
to pond design

FORMA

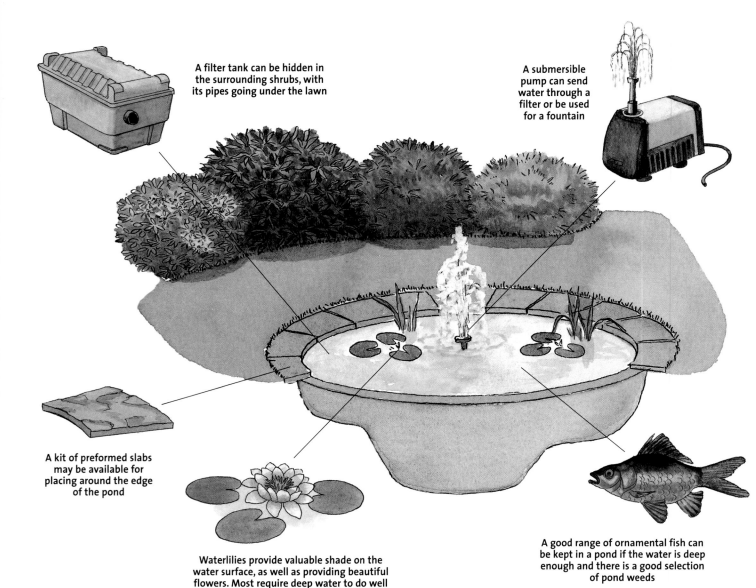

A filter tank can be hidden in
the surrounding shrubs, with
its pipes going under the lawn

A submersible
pump can send
water through a
filter or be used
for a fountain

A kit of preformed slabs
may be available for
placing around the edge
of the pond

Waterlilies provide valuable shade on the
water surface, as well as providing beautiful
flowers. Most require deep water to do well

A good range of ornamental fish can
be kept in a pond if the water is deep
enough and there is a good selection
of pond weeds

An ornamental fish pond is expected to support a selection of attractive fish, some ornamental planting and perhaps have a fountain. Some ornamental fish need quite deep water, so if the pond is not very large it may inevitably have steep sides.

Many ornamental fish ponds, though not all, are made from rigid materials such as plastic, glass fibre or concrete. Although some planting may be established on earth-filled shelves, most of the plants in a fish pond are grown in baskets of soil placed on shelves just beneath the water's surface or, in the case of some waterlilies and oxygenating weeds, placed on the bottom of the pond.

The pond edges are sometimes paved and surrounded, at least in part, by lawn. Others may be in a planted border with just stepping stones going up to the edge.

Clear water

There is an expectation for the water to be clear, partly so that the pond life remains visible, but also because ornamental fish prefer or need it to be so. To achieve this, a filter unit may be used. Some filtration units will need a tank, which can be hidden in bushes or partly buried in the ground.

The pipes are usually buried a little way under the ground. The pump may be fitted with an attachment which allows some water to be diverted up into a small fountain. Apart from its ornamental virtues, its action can also help to oxygenate the water.

Other than fish, the pond might have some snails and a few other creatures, but generally those associated with a muddier, more stagnant environment are not welcome, especially since some can introduce disease to the fish.

Planting can be very varied and therefore attract additional wildlife but, in general, a fish pond is a much clearer and cleaner feature than a wild pond.

Problems

Herons can be a nuisance, especially since some of the fish are often clearly visible and there is an edge for the bird to stand on. It may therefore be necessary to install some form of deterrent.

In the autumn, leaves and debris can spoil the clarity of the water – netting may be needed to stop leaves sinking to the bottom.

The wild pond

A wild pond sets out to mimic nature and provide a home for a wide range of native creatures which enjoy the often muddy, murky nature of a pond like this.

versus **WILD**

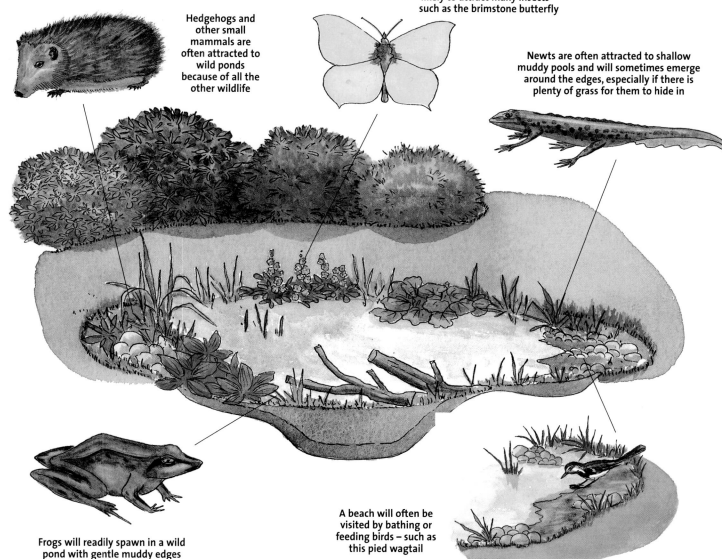

Wild flowers growing around the edge of a wild pond are likely to attract many insects – such as the brimstone butterfly

Hedgehogs and other small mammals are often attracted to wild ponds because of all the other wildlife

Newts are often attracted to shallow muddy pools and will sometimes emerge around the edges, especially if there is plenty of grass for them to hide in

Frogs will readily spawn in a wild pond with gentle muddy edges

A beach will often be visited by bathing or feeding birds – such as this pied wagtail

---

It is certainly not an ideal environment for ornamental fish, although natural species such as sticklebacks could thrive.

Most wild ponds are made from a liner – or possibly from puddled clay – and have very shallow sides. The central portion is often deeper, offering a degree of winter protection for its inhabitants.

Different environment

Because the sides are shallow they can often hold soil and therefore support a wide range of 'marginal' flowers and grasses. This gives many of the amphibious creatures, like frogs, toads and newts, an easily

concealed route in and out of the water.

Inevitably, muddy beaches are exposed when the water level drops and this provides feeding opportunities for many birds, bees, wasps, etc. Plants are rarely grown in baskets in a wild pond.

Although the water may become murky from time to time it is possible to achieve a balanced population of aquatic, oxygenating and marginal plants, as well as snails and other creatures to keep the water relatively clear for quite long periods.

A filter is rarely used and a fountain is often considered undesirable since it disturbs the surface of the water. This may discourage

some sections of wildlife.

An old log or two placed carefully on the edge can add character, as well as provide birds with a perch.

Varied animal life

This wild pond has been built in a lawn, but bushes and undergrowth should never be far away so that creatures do not have far to travel in the open, where they could fall prey to birds and other animals.

Most of the gently sloping sides will be covered in soil – and plants – but here and there a stony beach could replace these and provide birds with a firm place to bathe.

Planting is usually so successful on and around the edges of a wild pond that there is a danger of losing sight of the water altogether.

Once this happens, children and pets could be forgiven for thinking that the water is firm soil – with dire consequences!

Many insects will be attracted to the native – and other – flowers. Among these will be bees, butterflies, dragonflies and so on. In winter, most of the plants will die back and the pond can look quite messy.

It would, however, be a mistake to clear it all out since much of the debris is providing winter protection for animals.

An island in your pond provides an attractive habitat for wild creatures. Here are some effective ways to build one

Island sanctuary

If you are bored with how your pond is looking, then why not add an island? While the smallest of ponds might look silly with an even tinier island, many garden ponds are quite large enough to have one, and its presence will not just add visual interest but could provide many creatures – from ducks to newts – with an attractive habitat.

Exactly which creatures you attract will depend to some extent on how you plant the islands, and even what features you include.

Lush boggy conditions with lots of undergrowth will almost certainly encourage frogs, toads and newts.

A mounded, pebbly island with much sparser yet more exotic planting will probably attract small birds as well as give you your very own 'desert' island!

Larger islands might accommodate a simple shelter where ducks, coots or moorhens can roost, or perhaps even nest, well away from marauding cats and foxes.

Shaping

Depending upon the space available and the method of construction, the shape can vary from the simplest circular island to something far more extensive and interesting.

If space is available, the island might be elongated, curved, have low-lying waterlogged areas and other parts which are elevated and therefore drier. This factor alone helps to broaden the range of plants which can be grown within a small area.

Larger ponds could have an island which is nearer to one side than another, making it easy to span with a bridge – useful for some occasional maintenance but unwelcome if ducks are using the island as a safe haven.

Where it is likely to be difficult to add an island to an existing pond – perhaps because the pond would be damaged by construction or because it would be too disruptive to empty out most of the water, a simply designed floating island might be the answer.

Construction methods

There is no doubt that construction is easiest when it can take place in a totally empty pond. The presence of any water can be a hindrance, so before an established pond can be emptied, arrangements have to be made to provide temporary

ABOVE: A bridge links one side of this island on which a bare tree casts reflections on the water

This island is made from various rocky terraces. Some of the terraces would need some form of damp-proof membrane to reduce the amount of moisture rising upwards. These drier areas can then be planted with a wider range of plants, producing an ornate and interesting feature. Sterilised soil, at least in the top half of the island, helps to eliminate weeds. Some maintenance, mostly pruning, would be necessary from time to time

"The island might be elongated, curved, have low-lying waterlogged areas and other parts which are elevated and therefore drier"

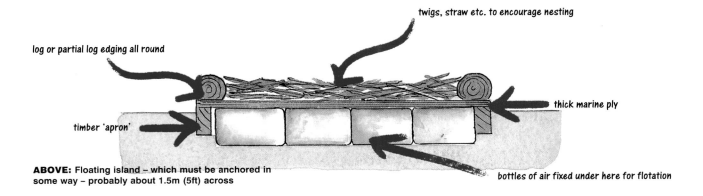

log or partial log edging all round

twigs, straw etc. to encourage nesting

thick marine ply

timber 'apron'

bottles of air fixed under here for flotation

ABOVE: Floating island – which must be anchored in some way – probably about 1.5m (5ft) across

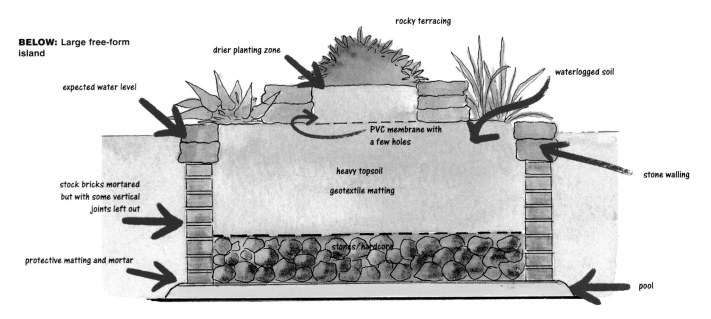

BELOW: Large free-form island

rocky terracing

drier planting zone

waterlogged soil

expected water level

PVC membrane with a few holes

heavy topsoil

geotextile matting

stone walling

stock bricks mortared but with some vertical joints left out

stones/hardcore

protective matting and mortar

pool

accommodation for fish and aquatic plants.

The base of the pond may also need protection from the traffic and construction which is about to take place.

The pond's suitability for an island must also be assessed.

A liner, for example, must have considerable cushioning from the weight of an island, either by using a geotextile underfelt or a generous bed of soft mortar. This may still not be enough to prevent sharp objects under the liner from causing damage. Likewise, moulded fibreglass, and especially rigid plastic ponds, could split under the extra weight if they have not been properly packed out underneath. Even concrete, if not reinforced, may be at risk.

Prefabricated island

One of the simplest methods of construction is to use a large pre-formed round or square plastic water tank which has been given plenty of holes and cut down, if necessary, to just below the lowest likely water level so that it does not show.

It is put in position on top of some protective matting or mortar and partly filled with hardcore, preferably stones or broken bricks – broken concrete could contaminate the water with excessive amounts of lime.

On top of the hardcore goes soil – preferably a weed-free heavy loam but, since this will have to rise above the highest water level, the sides of the tank must be extended with something which will not look unattractive when the water level drops.

Vertical strips or planks of timber can be arranged around the inside of the tank and extending upwards the appropriate amount.

Strips of oak from a couple of oak tubs would be ideal since they are unlikely to have been impregnated with any toxic substances.

Geotextile matting can be used to line the inside so that packed-in soil does not seep out between any small gaps that could have developed between

BELOW: Small prefabricated island can be round or rectangular

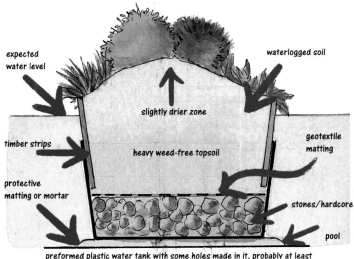

expected water level

waterlogged soil

slightly drier zone

timber strips

geotextile matting

heavy weed-free topsoil

protective matting or mortar

stones/hardcore

pool

preformed plastic water tank with some holes made in it, probably at least 1m (3ft 3in) across, depending on tank size

Built largely within a large water tank, this island, though quite small, has been split into two halves by a gorge going from one side to the other. All the plants will have to tolerate, or thrive in, very wet soil, and very tall or vigorous plants must be avoided. The island of a pond situated close to the house could also serve as a bird bath

Planting for effect

Any flat or beach-like areas could have Hottonia palustris (water violet) planted close by in the water so that it invades part of the flat area. Other possibilities here are Acorus gramineus 'Variegatus', a small variegated grass, Calla palustris (bog arum), Hydrocotyle vulgaris , a creeping plant with small white flowers, Lysimachia nummularia 'Aurea', a relatively non-invasive golden form of creeping Jenny, and, perhaps Ajuga reptans 'Atropurpurea'.

In other parts of the island some taller planting could be possible, including rushes and grasses, shrubs like the coloured stemmed dogwoods and shrubby willows along with a small tree or two, like Alnus incana 'Aurea' and, on a drier island, Betula pendula 'Youngii'. Very small weeping trees, though beautiful, can easily be swamped by the surrounding plants.

the planks of wood.

On no account should pressure-treated timber be used in this or any other water project as the treatment chemicals could leach out into the water and poison the pond life.

The soil can be mounded slightly so that the central area is just a little drier than the rest, but too much of a mound could become eroded in heavy rain and look odd.

Larger islands

Where space and pool strength allow, a much more interesting island could be created.

With an interesting shape mapped out on the floor of the pool, the lower half can be built up using bricks or maybe sand bags – with adequate protection for the pool. Concrete blocks are a possibility, but these may,

initially at least, raise the alkalinity of the water too high.

As the walls rise up to near the lowest likely water level, so more attractive construction materials take over from the mundane – stone, rocks etc.

If space allows, some parts of the island should be just below the average water level so that it is possible to bring soil up and out of the water to form a beach.

Other parts of the island might be built up much higher in the form of rocky terraces or cliffs to resemble coves and bays around the beaches.

The fact that on some occa-

sions the water level will be lower or higher than on others will add to the interest – so long as the mundane walling is never visible.

Although the use of concrete blocks for construction can easily be avoided, along with broken concrete in any hardcore, the use of mortar alone could increase the pond alkalinity for a while.

If this is not acceptable then some form of 'dry' walling can be used, but only if the walls are given a batter – a backward lean – for stability.

If stone walling is used, then a hard stone which is not especially alkaline is best. To prevent erosion and damage by waterfowl, use large pieces at the top.

> "One of the simplest methods of construction is to use a large pre-formed round or square plastic water tank"

A plinth must be provided on one side to accommodate a bridge. Lighting or a pump for moving water requires a suitable power supply and sockets.

Once again, the island can be backfilled first with hardcore, followed by a heavy weed-free loam. If any areas are to be kept relatively dry, a PVC membrane could be incorporated so that water cannot rise up from the saturated area below.

A few holes in this membrane allow limited upward movement of water, whereas areas with no membrane are likely to be constantly damp. The regime can be tailored to suit the planned planting.

Floating islands

It is tricky to get these right: too much sodden timber and they

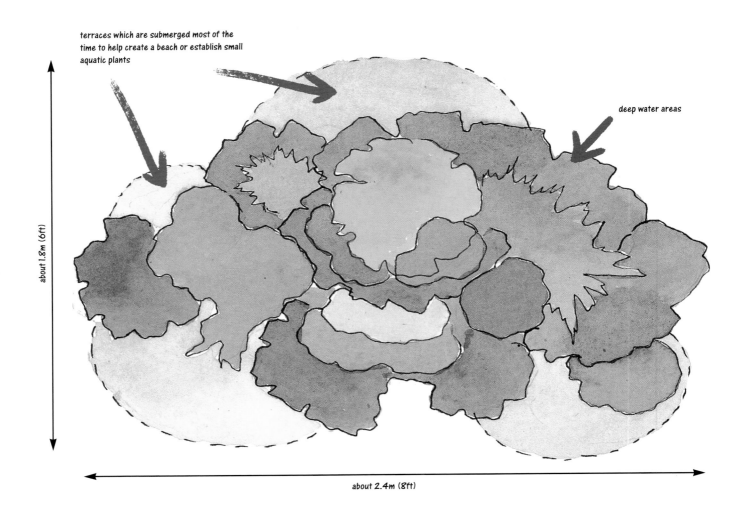

terraces which are submerged most of the time to help create a beach or establish small aquatic plants

deep water areas

about 1.8m (6ft)

about 2.4m (8ft)

can all but sink; too much flotation and they can look like a cork bobbing around on the surface. Simplicity is usually the answer.

The most convincing form of floating island is a nesting raft with a shallow bed of twigs and straw – perhaps even a second-hand moorhen's nest – floating in a situation where waterfowl may be tempted to use it.

Any soil and planting is likely to become too heavy. Most floating 'islands' are made from various forms of non-impregnated timbers. These might include a raft of marine ply, an edging of hardwood logs/branches and space for canisters or bottles of air beneath.

Island dimensions, types of timber, the number of flotation

bottles etc. are all likely to be somewhat experimental – there are too many variables to plan with any certainty.

Aiming to stun

Soil conditions and moisture content will influence the selection of plants and this in turn will give the island its character. Disproportionate planting can look silly; flat areas lose their identity under tall planting – creeping or dwarf plants are best here.

Raised areas can be accentuated by the use of small trees or conifers – possibly even a small weeping tree. Freedom to select from a whole range of plants can only be possible if some areas are moist and others are relatively dry.

The possibilities are almost

"The most convincing form of floating island is a nesting raft with a shallow bed of twigs and straw"

endless, but the secret of success is to aim for a particular effect so that you design, build and plant accordingly – for stunning results!

Exotic look

Many of the following plants would prefer soil which was not constantly wet or waterlogged. Some are not totally hardy, and wet soil would exacerbate their lack of hardiness.

Chamaerops humilis is a dwarf bushy but spreading palm which could completely cover an island 1.8m (6ft) across. Other possibilities include phormium, cordyline, yucca,

Fatsia japonica 'Variegata', *Pinus mugo* and many small ornamental grasses.

Oriental theme

Here, small trees like Japanese maples, weeping cherries and *Caragana arborescens* 'Walker' can be very effective. On a slightly larger scale, *Rhus typhina* 'Laciniata' and aralias can also look good, especially in conjunction with rounded boulders, pebbles and gravel.

Again, dwarf grasses and bamboos can be used, perhaps along with totally prostrate plants, especially junipers.

ways of making it both attractive and accessible to many creatures. It therefore helps to know what features are likely to prove the most attractive.

Plant life

A good dense population of reeds, grasses, bog and marginal plants will provide cover for frogs, toads, newts and beetles as well as dragonflies, moths and butterflies. This type of planting is unlikely to thrive under the overhang of a large tree – an open, fairly sunny spot is best, adjacent to a lot of existing undergrowth so that there is a continuous source of cover from the water's edge into the rest of the garden. A few small shrub plants, and perhaps a dead branch suspended out across the water will provide somewhere for birds to perch.

Generally speaking, 'still' water is preferable to any vigorous fountain or cascade, although a slow flowing stream is alright. Without movement and filtration, the pond will rely on plenty of aquatic and oxygenating plants to keep the water healthy.

Shaping banks

Gentle 'beaches' going initially into shallow water suit most visitors to the water's edge. This also encourages the growth of marginal plants, most of which thrive in boggy soil with only a

Wildlife pond

Some further suggestions for attracting wildlife to your water garden

TOP: Diverse wildlife will visit the right sort of pond – here a common darter dragonfly drops in on a waterlily

LEFT: Frogs congregate round frogspawn

I t is not difficult to encourage wildlife into the garden and quite often it is already there, but the right sort of pond can attract a whole range of creatures from even further afield, especially if yours is the only pond in the neighbourhood.

Although it is amazing how resourceful frogs can be at getting into the most difficult ponds, when you create a wildlife pond from scratch there are various

Warning:
Remember,
this is not a
child-safe
water feature

thick geotextile
underlay

butyl liner

VIEWING PLATFORMS

It is a good idea to have a seat or bench – perhaps placed to catch the evening sun – from where all the activity can be watched. However, if you want to peer into the water at close quarters you will need some form of viewing platform. This might be in the form of decking, perhaps cantilevered out over the water or, as illustrated, a zig-zag walkway going between separate or linked areas of water. Any platform must be strong and well balanced so that it does not become unstable when you kneel on the edge to look into the water.

ABOVE: A timber walkway makes a good viewing platform from which to watch wildlife

BRIAN BEVAN

shallow covering of water. Where a beach slopes only slightly down towards the sea, a lot of the beach is exposed at low tide. The same can happen if water evaporates from the pond, so its 'beach' must be created in a way that ensures that even at 'low

tide' it does not lose contact with the main body of water. A pond edge with some deep indentations or creeks will be more attractive to pond life than one which is plain and featureless.

Water depth

While the edges of the pond should have shallow water, there should be some areas in the centre which are much deeper – some creatures need a depth of 60cm (2ft).

Deep water can of course spell danger for young children, pets and many small mammals. A 'beach' section can sometimes warn small mammals that the water is

getting deeper and therefore put them off travelling further.

Size

Almost any size of pond can be made to work – I had a wildlife pond that was only 1.2m (4ft) across and 1.5m (5ft) long. The water remained remarkably clear, beneath a canopy of floating weed, and there were often 20 or more birds visiting at any one time! It wasn't until I had a day off work that I realised that all these birds bathing resulted in a huge water-loss – a problem in a small pool where its capacity is not very great to start with.

Another problem with a small

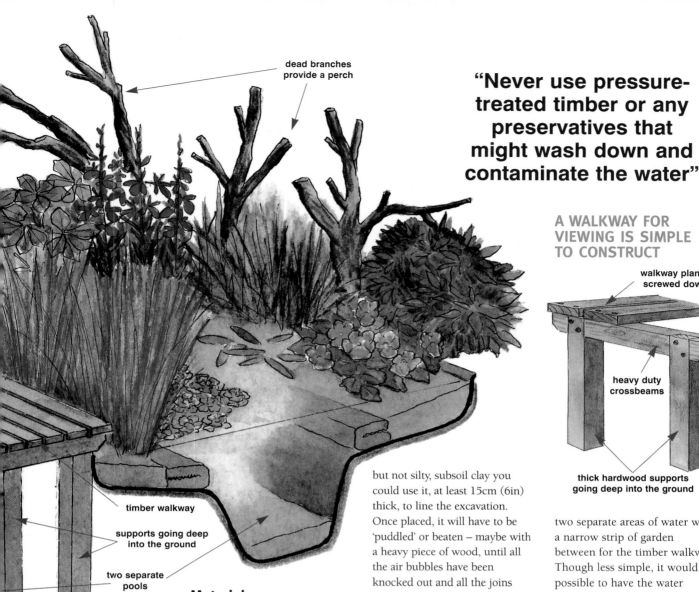

dead branches provide a perch

timber walkway

supports going deep into the ground

two separate pools

A WALKWAY FOR VIEWING IS SIMPLE TO CONSTRUCT

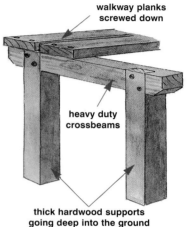

walkway planks screwed down

heavy duty crossbeams

thick hardwood supports going deep into the ground

pond is that floating weeds can form such a dense cover that it can look like the lawn or border. A young child ran straight into ours one day, believing it to be solid ground!

the liner must protrude by about 1cm (½in)

soil filled shelf

garden soil

thick underfelt

old, dead turf

deep part

A SOLUTION FOR STABLE SOIL

liner must remain protruding

soft filled shelf

extra thick underfelt

whole or half bricks

thick geotextile underfelt

A SOLUTION FOR UNSTABLE SOIL

Materials

The most realistic and suitable option for the lining of the pond is probably a butyl liner although reinforced PVC liners can be used as they will not be exposed to UV light. A liner must always be used in conjunction with an underfelt and be given additional protection from any soil placed on top.

Rendered concrete could be used, but for this type of project it would be a rather clumsy option, especially around the edges. Another possibility is puddled clay. If you have some very pure,

but not silty, subsoil clay you could use it, at least 15cm (6in) thick, to line the excavation. Once placed, it will have to be 'puddled' or beaten – maybe with a heavy piece of wood, until all the air bubbles have been knocked out and all the joins have disappeared – rather like preparing clay for a potter's kiln. While puddled clay was once the most common way of lining a pond, it can be rather hit and miss and is not really suitable for small ponds where drying out might result in cracking.

Moulded fibreglass ponds can be made to work but are much more restricting than a liner.

Construction

A reasonably level site is needed, away from the overhang of any large trees. In a project like the one illustrated there are in fact

two separate areas of water with a narrow strip of garden between for the timber walkway. Though less simple, it would be possible to have the water continuous at one point between the two main areas, as long as it was still possible to support the walkway without having to put supports down onto the liner.

The more complicated you make the shape for a liner, the more folds you will have to accommodate.

Shallow areas

Shallow areas are created from shelves which must be cut vertically 15cm (6in) down at the edge, then sloped gently down towards the centre of the pond.

Deep section

The central part of the pond needs to be deeper. If, during excavation, the edges of this deeper section begin to crumble – typically in light soil – some strengthening will be necessary. This could be done with bricks stacked dry on top of one another. They could also go one brick higher than the edge of

A GENTLE 'BEACH' WILL ATTRACT MORE WILDLIFE AND CAN BE PLANTED WITH MARGINAL PLANTS

"A 'beach' section can sometimes warn small mammals that the water is getting deeper and therefore put them off travelling further"

the shelf so that they produce a small hump in the liner which will prevent soil on the shallow shelf from washing down into the deeper part. This extra support may not be needed in clay or chalk. The whole excavation must be lined with a geotextile underfelt with extra layers placed over any blocks, bricks or other sharp objects.

Timber walkway
Perhaps the easiest way to support a timber walkway is on pairs of oak posts going deep into the soil between the areas of water with a cross-bar joining them. Planks can then be screwed down onto these crossbars, leaving a small gap between each. The distance between these supports will depend upon the thickness of the planks and how many changes in direction there are. Never use pressure-treated timber or any preservatives that might wash down and contaminate the water. Hardwood planks are ideal.

Placing liner
The liner should be placed as centrally as possible, then put about 5cm (2in) of stone-free

heavy or clay soil on top in the deep section to weigh it down, but not so much as to make it impossible to adjust the liner's position if necessary.

Once the liner has been adjusted and the creases evened out as much as possible, a little more soil can be added and compacted before water is introduced almost up as far as the shelf. Where bricks have been used under the liner to form a restraint, soil can be added to the shelf so that it fills the area right back to the outer edges where the liner emerges vertically, and to the level of the surrounding garden. At this point, soil on the shelf will be about 15cm (6in) deep. Where bricks or blocks have not been used, old dead turf folded over can be placed close to, but not right on, the edge of the shallow shelf to hold back this soil. All the soil must be free from sharp stones, be 'heavy' and well compacted.

RIGHT: Brown hawker dragonfly reflected in the clear water of a pond

BRIAN BEVAN

The pond can now be filled and excess liner trimmed off, but about 1cm (½in) must be left protruding vertically from the soil all round to act as a damp-proof membrane.

Planting
The general theme for planting could be entirely 'native',

ornamental, or a mixture. This will have little bearing on the visiting wildlife, except perhaps in terms of insect life. In the deep part, plant various floating and oxygenating weeds with possibly a waterlily or two in larger ponds.

On the shallow shelves plant small grasses, sedges, water forget-me-not, primulas and other marginal plants up to perhaps 45cm (18in) tall.

In the surrounding garden you could have plants like hostas, astilbes, rodgersia and irises – all those plants which are often considered as 'bog' plants but which can tolerate this drier area. Any shrubs or small trees should be kept at least 2m (6ft 6in) away so that their roots do not damage the liner. Avoid planting bamboos or anything else with sharp underground stems, including *Helictotrichon sempervirens*, close to the liner.

Wildlife at Isabella Plantation,
Richmond Park, Surrey

Shady glade

ABOVE: There are only two original mature trees here. All the other plants have been planted within the last few years and mature plants and trees in the neighbouring garden help to give an overall impression of maturity. Overhead leaf canopies are quite high and not especially dense, so a good range of plants can thrive

which prevent me from growing a wide range of plants in the glade – just shrubs and grasses, but even so it is still a lovely feature. Most people do not have this problem, and can grow a whole range of interesting woodland plants.

Definition

A glade is defined as a clearing in the trees. If you have no trees of your own, this could mean that you have the clearing and your neighbours have the trees which in some ways might give you the best of both worlds. Although your neighbour's trees and shrubs may form the backdrop for your glade, one or two well-established trees of your own will certainly help to give the glade a feeling of maturity. Too many trees on the other hand, especially those with large leaves like horse chestnut, can make it almost impossible for other plants to survive, so a lightly wooded situation offers the most potential.

Developing a glade

My glade has developed over the years, more or less naturally but with just a little help from me. Initially it was waist deep in bracken and nothing else

> **" The glade is a wonderful place to sit, especially on a hot sunny day or during warm summer evenings "**

had a chance. I managed to kill off the bracken with herbicide and as the bracken receded, so natural grasses began to move in. At first these grew in a narrow ribbon through part of the glade so I started to mow it regularly, with the grass box off. Initially this was difficult and the ground was spongy but gradually the area of grass spread. Most was cut regularly but other areas were allowed to grow wild in the hope that other plants would develop. Even during the driest weather the grass survives, probably because it is nature's own natural selection for a wood. Some moss develops each winter to help turn it into an emerald carpet. Each summer wild foxgloves seed themselves in great numbers where the grass is longer and a few other wild flowers come and go but our soil is acid and this limits the potential.

If you prefer to develop your glade along these more naturalistic lines,

The joys of a woodland glade are unequalled at any time of year – and you can create one even in a small garden

One of the greatest pleasures I have from my garden is to walk through the woodland glade at different times of the year. In winter it can be adorned with frost or snow, while in spring and autumn shafts of sunlight cut through the early morning mists. There is always a selection of birds to watch and occasionally deer pass through looking for the juicy tips of brambles. It is these particular visitors

Steps

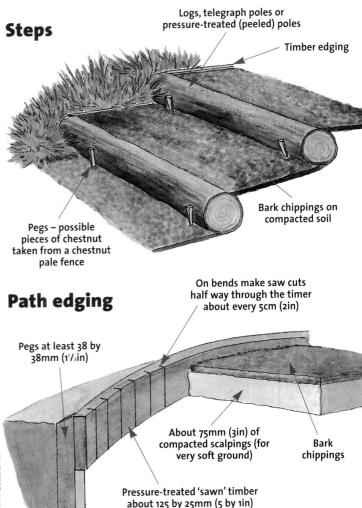

Logs, telegraph poles or pressure-treated (peeled) poles

Timber edging

Bark chippings on compacted soil

Pegs – possible pieces of chestnut taken from a chestnut pale fence

Path edging

On bends make saw cuts half way through the timer about every 5cm (2in)

Pegs at least 38 by 38mm (1¹/₂in)

About 75mm (3in) of compacted scalpings (for very soft ground)

Bark chippings

Pressure-treated 'sawn' timber about 125 by 25mm (5 by 1in)

HARRY SMITH COLLECTION

ABOVE: Spring is a wonderful time for wild flowers in a glade

whether or not you have deer and rabbits, you could introduce various ornamental grasses, many of which are both attractive yet 'wild' looking. I have some Bowles golden grass which has crept in among the others and, despite its soft yellow leaves, it doesn't look out of place, although variegated or striped grasses might. If you need to start from scratch with some grass, you will need what is labelled as 'shade or woodland' seed mixture. This is not designed to create a lawn but something much more akin to a glade floor.

Paths

A path adds interest to a glade. Bark chippings, 5cm (2in) deep, within timber edging are ideal. The timber edging can be sawn or have a rustic look but must be pressure-treated

> **There is always a selection of birds to watch and occasionally deer pass through looking for the juicy tips of brambles**

against decay. If you edge your paths with old branches or logs there is a likelihood that honey fungus could be brought in on them and then go on to infect nearby plants.

Since the use of these paths is usually only occasional, the bark can go straight onto well-compacted soil – compact the soil with a 'vibrating plate'. In boggy areas, the paths could be made from well-compacted scalpings, 75mm (3in) laid between timber edging, with or without bark chippings over the top.

Tree stumps

You can sometimes find old stumps with lots of character lying around under trees. Importing some of these and making them look as if they have always been there can add character and provide somewhere for ferns or even miniature cyclamen to grow. However, the problem of honey fungus exists here too, so the stumps should be first thoroughly treated with a broad spectrum, colourless preservative.

Stream or ditch

The problem with any area of water lying under trees is that it can become

clogged with leaves. These will quickly block any submersible pump which is being used to circulate the water, and on balance it is probably best not to involve a pump in this situation. It will mean that the water will stagnate and become something of a bog rather than a clear pool or 'stream', but it will still support a selection of shade-tolerant bog plants as well as creatures like frogs, toads and newts, and sometimes snakes.

Bridge

With a long narrow stretch of water can come a bridge, or two. Rather than being highly ornate, this will look more in keeping if kept simple – perhaps some thick planks of wood or railway sleepers fixed together underneath with some battens, again pressure-treated.

Steps

Although many glades occupy relatively level sites they can of course be on a slope, perhaps with a series of broad steps joining one area with another. Despite the threat of honey fungus, log steps are one possibility. Another option is to purchase thick, peeled, pressure-

A boggy ditch

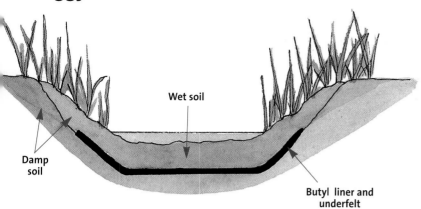

Wet soil

Damp soil

Butyl liner and underfelt

A static stream for aquatic and bog plants

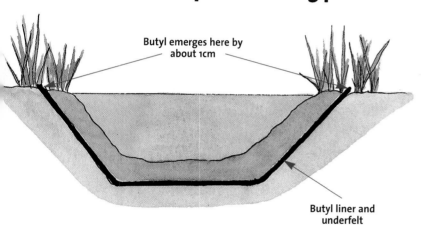

Butyl emerges here by about 1cm

Butyl liner and underfelt

treated poles or, on a larger scale, use old telegraph poles which, like sleepers, are tar impregnated.

Seating
The glade is a wonderful place to sit, especially on a hot sunny day or during warm summer evenings. A simple bench made from a thick plank fixed down onto two stumps will look much more 'natural' than a highly ornate garden seat.

Lighting
There are lots of possibilities when it comes to lighting, from low level lights just illuminating a path, to high voltage/wattage floodlights lighting up whole trees. You may not consider lighting worth including if the glade is a long way from the house, but where it is close by, lighting can bring it into the general 'nightscape' of the garden so it can be admired from within the house or conservatory.

CCTV
If your glade becomes home to foxes, badgers and other wildlife, you could watch some of this from the comfort of your armchair by using TV cameras and, at night, infra-red cameras linked direct to your television. It is possible to have these tuned in to one particular channel so that you can easily switch across and see what is going on.

Flowers
Parts of the glade will probably be grassed while other parts may be just bare earth or humus. Many spring flowers come from bulbs, like narcissi, snowdrops, crocuses and so on. It will be important to ensure that the taller flowers come up in the grass while the smallest are given the more open, less overgrown places. In the autumn, colchicum – the autumn crocus – will need the support of fairly short grasses so that the flowers are not squashed flat on the ground by heavy rain. Other useful flowers include: hellebore, pulmonaria, brunnera, liriope, foxglove, aquilegia, and where the cover of trees is not too dense, geranium. Autumn colour can come from Japanese maples, amelanchier, parrotia, sorbus, *Euonymus europaeus* and so on.

Trees and shrubs

It will obviously be useful if your neighbours do have trees and shrubs close to your boundary, but there may be nothing apart from a couple of trees in your own garden, so you will need to create a piece of woodland before you can achieve any sort of glade. Most woodland trees take years to develop but there are some trees which grow quite quickly, without becoming huge, and there are some shrubs which, left untrimmed, will also soon grow into small trees. Examples of these are: amelanchier, arbutus, corylus, *Cotoneaster sternianus, C. rothschildianus*, and *C. cornubia, Genista aetnensis*, halesia, hamamelis (acid soil), ligustrum, *Philadelphus virginalis*, photinia, *Prunus laurocerasus* (laurel), *Prunus lusitanica, Rhus typhina*, salix (various), sambucus (elder), *Spartium junceum*, syringa (lilac), *Viburnum opulus*.

If you want these plants to establish and grow quickly, it will be important to prepare the soil well, incorporate some well-rotted compost or manure and water during their first summer. This is especially important if you already have some mature trees close by.

In addition to some of these 'small' trees, you should add some other fairly large evergreen shrubs, mainly along the boundaries. Conifers, except pines, tend to look a little out of place in a woodland setting. If your neighbours do indeed have a lot of tall planting alongside their boundary, you can often make it look like part of yours by planting densely along your side and thus hiding any fence. There is no need to do this if the boundary is a natural-looking hedge – just let your side grow out of hand!

> ❝ *Each summer wild foxgloves seed themselves in great numbers where the grass is longer and a few other wild flowers come and go* ❞

Plants that tolerate dry and shady areas

All the following plants would *prefer* some light and moisture but are remarkably tolerant of poor conditions, so you could try some of these if all else fails!

Bergenia, brunnera, cortaderia, epimedium, some ferns, *Iris foetidissima*, lamium (but it is invasive), liriope, pachysandra, pulmonaria and trachystemon.

There are also many shrubs which tolerate dry and shady conditions, including:

Arundinaria, buxus, euonymus, hedera, ilex, mahonia, *Ribes sanguineum, Ruscus aculeatus*, sarcococca, skimmia, symphoricarpos, and vinca.

All are more likely to succeed if they are given good planting conditions including deeply cultivated soil, well-rotted manure and some initial watering.

Con

Naturalness is the keyword to making a successful stream – but careful planning is essential too

● PICTURES: HARRY SMITH COLLECTION

Many of the water features we set out to create in our gardens are intended to appear natural. Most, of course, stand little chance of appearing so, having to be squeezed up against a garden shed or a fence, under a tree, next to a garage and so on.

A 'stream' does, however, stand a good chance of succeeding where other water features might fail because, after all, it is only a strip of water going from A to B, and these do occur naturally in all manner of situations.

Stream types

Real streams appear and disappear so an artificial one must be given a plausible beginning and end.

I have sometimes walked down the high street of a market town and been fascinated by a gurgling gully running alongside the pavement, wanting to see where it emerges, where it disappears to and to guess where it goes to after that.

As even this gurgling gully could be regarded as a natural phenomenon despite the fact

This bridged stream has no obvious beginning or end and its banks hang heavy with lush plantings

ng on stream

ABOVE: Natural plantings by this stream are right for the wild Scottish setting on the Isle of Mull

ABOVE: This stream is set off by the gently curving path above, balanced by the bank which slopes down from the path, and enhanced by the beauty of primulas

that it is running in a man-made rill, it not unreasonable to decide to mimic any water course from meadow brook to rocky stream.

For the gurgling gully could easily fit into a courtyard, a meadow brook across a flat grass area and a rocky stream could have a place close to a convincing rock garden or embankment.

Behind the scenes

In all cases, of course, the water will be circulated by a pump. This would normally be 'submersible' – staying under water – pushing water to wherever it is needed.

The water has, therefore, to be piped to the 'top end' and collected by the pump at the 'bottom' where the water must be deep enough to accommodate the pump and to ensure that the system never runs dry.

The terms 'top end' and 'bottom end' are in fact inappropriate because in nearly all cases an artificial stream is made dead level so that it remains full once the pump has been turned off.

It does, at that point, become an elongated pool. The flow comes from sucking the water out at one end and pushing it back in at the other. Pumps obviously vary enormously in their performance, and it is vital to match a pump with the overall effect wanted. A small pump in a very wide or deep stream would produce an imperceptible and completely ineffective flow.

Choosing a pump

It takes a surprisingly powerful pump to recreate the gurgling gully. The flow of water may be no deeper than 15cm (6in) and no wider than, say, 30cm (12in), but the flow is quite vigorous – usually because the water is being fed in from a nearby hillside.

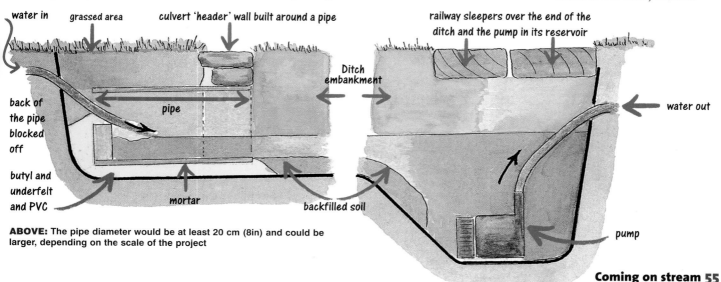

water in grassed area culvert 'header' wall built around a pipe

railway sleepers over the end of the ditch and the pump in its reservoir

Ditch embankment

back of the pipe blocked off

pipe

water out

butyl and underfelt and PVC

mortar

backfilled soil

pump

ABOVE: The pipe diameter would be at least 20 cm (8in) and could be larger, depending on the scale of the project

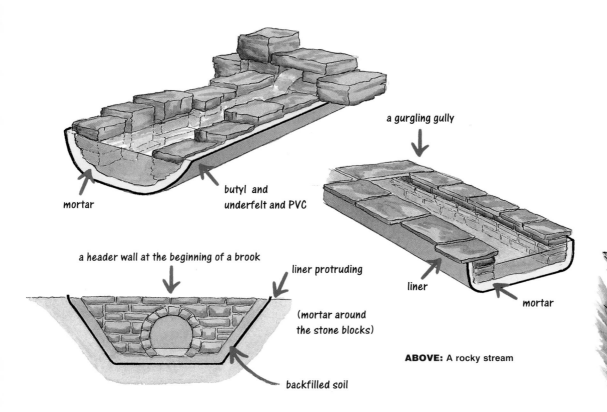

mortar

butyl and
underfelt and PVC

a header wall at the beginning of a brook

liner protruding

(mortar around
the stone blocks)

backfilled soil

a gurgling gully

liner

mortar

ABOVE: A rocky stream

A meadow brook is usually wider and often runs in the bottom of a ditch. While the water could be as much as 90cm (3ft) wide, it may only be 15 to 25cm (6 to 9in) deep.

The flow here is usually steady but seldom frantic – mainly because the surrounding land is often relatively flat. It will certainly be steady enough to cause the fronds of any aquatic plants to move significantly with the current.

Once again, quite a powerful pump is needed. The flow in a rocky stream varies considerably in 'the wild', depending upon its size and the 'head' of water

feeding it. This leaves the choice of effect wide open – from a small bubbling stream to a gushing torrent bursting through rocks and boulders. Perhaps this latter effect would look silly in a tiny rock garden!

Almost any size of pump can therefore be used for the rocky stream but, taking all these projects as a whole, the best policy is usually to use the largest pump you can accommodate and fit a valve to control the flow.

Beginning and end

Gurgling gullies tend to emerge from pipes, small tunnels

(culverts) or from beneath a stone slab, and disappear in much the same way. Most gullies are built from stone or brick and are therefore rigid and, in the main, straight or only gently curving.

Any abrupt change of direction should be made with the help of a covered chamber so that water can enter from one direction and leave at another.

Such a chamber could also be used to end the gully.

Meadow brooks also emerge from and disappear into pipes – often quite large ones – but also flow through tunnels and culverts which can be built from stone or brick.

In a flat garden all this can only really be achieved by setting the whole feature below ground level so that the brook runs along the bottom of a ditch – at least 45 to 60cm (18 to 24in) deep.

Since a brook often meanders its way through an area of grass or lawn, it tends to be a feature that you come across and may only be detectable from a distance by a ribbon of tall marginal plants interrupting the

expanse of grass.

Mowing access from one side to the other could be important, but this can usually be provided by a bridge or by having a section of the brook piped underground.

A bridge can sometimes be used as an effective way of beginning or ending a brook. Rock streams nearly always emerge from a pile of rocks or from a crevice in a rock face.

They often disappear in a similar manner or beneath a large piece of stone – where a

ABOVE: Stream with stepping stones

planting has been done with common waterside grasses and wildflowers

ABOVE: A strong flow of water is fed in at the back of the pipe. Stones placed in the way of the flow create some extra movement. The whole feature is built within a butyl liner – nature does the rest

pump and reservoir could be housed.

Rock streams can be made to change direction quite suddenly with sometimes dramatic effects, but there is a danger that water can be lost from the system if it splashes too violently.

Overall it is, therefore, important to choose the type of stream which is most likely to fit well into the available surroundings, to decide on how vigorous the flow of water needs to be, the route it must take and how it should begin and end.

The right combination can produce a remarkably realistic effect under the most restricted circumstances, provided of course that the actual construction has been carried out convincingly too.

Gullies and rills

Although man-made in one sense, gullies and rills do conduct a 'natural' flow of water and can, therefore, be made to look reasonably natural.

A butyl liner must be contin-uous from one end to the other, and contain the whole construc-tion.

An underfelt and, perhaps, a layer of soft sand, must first go under the liner, with a layer of black 500-gauge PVC laid on top.

The gully will, in effect, be formed between two stone or brick walls bedded carefully onto a generous layer of soft-sand mortar. This can extend across the floor of the gully to a depth of about 2.5cm (1in), so that the liner is completely hidden.

The chosen beginning and end of the gully must also be built within the liner. Only those parts which will not come into contact with the water can extend beyond.

One area of the gully – at the exit end – must be deeper, to accommodate a pump along with a concealed reservoir.

Pebbles and stones set into the bottom of the gully can create some interesting effects, especially if the water flow is quite shallow. If the gully runs

"The flow comes from sucking the water out at one end and pushing it back in at the other"

through an area of paving with little or no adjacent planting, some thought must be given to ascertain how best to arrange a discreet connection to an electricity supply.

Meadow brook

As before, a continuous liner must be laid from one end to the other. Construction will be taking place within a ditch with banks no steeper than about 45°.

A quantity of soil will be going back on top of the liner so the ditch must be made some 10cm (4in) deeper and wider in all directions to accommodate this.

If the brook is to be planted with lots of marginal and aquatic plants then it should be made wider still so that at the height of summer these plants do not completely hide the fact that there is running water.

The brook could end up at least 90cm (3ft) wide. Once again, a liner must be used in conjunction with an underfelt and a top layer of PVC, and embrace both ends of the scheme.

Again, the pump must have a good-sized reservoir, if not a pond. The flow can be accentuated by having some rounded boulders – or some other plausi-

ble obstruction – blocking the flow so that water has to force its way past and therefore create a more perceptible flow.

Once the two ends have been constructed the liner can be covered from one end to the other by the 10cm (4in) or so of soil.

With banks as steep as 45° a heavy clay soil will be more stable than anything lighter. If clay is not available then two layers of dead, upturned turf could be used although it may be more difficult to plant into this.

It is vital that this 'internal' soil never makes contact with the surrounding garden soil. If it does, water will be constantly 'sucked' out of the feature. To this end, a narrow strip of liner – about 1cm ($^{3}/_{8}$in) – should remain visible all round.

This will probably be quite high up on the bank and will, in time, be hidden by grasses and any marginal planting.

Rock streams

Rock streams can be built in the same way as a gully. Rocks can be sharp, so generous amounts of mortar should be used within the liner to protect it.

Since some rocks might be quite large, the butyl-lined

excavation must be wide enough to ensure that once the rocks are in place there is still room for a reasonable width of stream.

If there is no pool at the bottom end then once again the pump must be housed in a

generous reservoir.

This, and all the other streams, must, above all else, be made level – not sloping – so that they remain full and looking reasonable, even once the pump is turned off.

ABOVE: Careful placing of cobblestones along the edges of this stream emphasise its length and the slight movement of the water

A peaceful stream in the Tranquillity garden,
Hampton Court Flower Show, 1999

The formal Italian gardens at Compton Acres are magnificent – but you can give even a small space the same flavour

Strictly
formal

There's nothing like a touch of formality to add style and grace to a garden – and it need not be difficult to achieve

There is a tendency these days for gardens, and their pools, to be created along informal lines but formal pools can look wonderful, even in quite a small garden.

You will see on the following pages how I have designed both a formal pool and a formal garden, both of which have curves that are so easy on the eye.

Practicalities

To tell the truth, I designed the pond first and created the garden around it so that they would complement one another.

There are not many paving options available which will allow you to create curved ends to a pool, but if you open a paving brochure you are almost bound to come across some circle kits which are designed to create circular patios. Many

CHRIS SKARBON

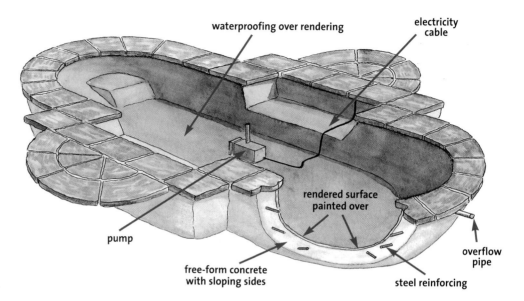

waterproofing over rendering

electricity cable

rendered surface painted over

pump

free-form concrete with sloping sides

steel reinforcing

overflow pipe

of these circles are made up from at least two complete circles of wedge-shaped slabs and some of the larger kits use three or four circles. It therefore makes sense to design the pond around these since they work out a lot less expensive than having stone coping specially cut.

My pond uses a kit of three circles, the outer one having a diameter of 2.7m (9ft) but you could just as easily use a much smaller kit based on just two circles, giving a maximum diameter of only about 1.8m (6ft). I have used the largest circle of slabs to form the two semicircular ends, and the remaining two circles, together, to form the two semicircular paved areas on either side. If you were to use the much smaller two-circle kit, the outer circle would, as before, form the two semi-circular ends and the single inner circle would be used for two small paved semi-circles on either side.

Positioning

As a formal pool, it must sit comfortably within a reasonably large open space and, if possible, line up with a view or vista from the house. Ideally it should not be too far from the house or from a seat so that it can be enjoyed for as many weeks of the year as possible. In my example I have placed the pool precisely in the centre of a formal lawn surrounded by dwarf hedges and borders. A lot of formal lawns can prove difficult to mow because the mower cannot reach into all the corners but here paths enter the lawn at critical points to make mowing easy. The area must be perfectly level and open to the air and sun, and not overhung by trees.

It will need an electricity supply and somewhere for an overflow pipe to discharge water from time to time.

Building options

There are three main ways in which you can build this type of pool:
1 By laying a thick steel reinforced base, then building up double-skinned walls with the steel running up from the base into the cavities. Bricks are used for the curved sections and concrete blocks for the straight lengths. The cavities would be packed with some concrete or mortar and the inside of the whole structure rendered to make it waterproof.
2 Alternatively, you could lay a concrete base as before, but make it a little less substantial. Build up single-skin walls, without reinforcing, then

line the whole structure with a pre-shaped butyl liner. Water garden specialists who sell butyl can usually arrange to have the liner made to the shape but they would need a detailed drawing of the pond and measurements to work to. The liner has to be laid over a thick under-felt to protect it from sharp edges, and have a flap all around the top to anchor it under the coping stones.
3 The third option is to use free-form concrete, and steel reinforcing, to create a pool shape with slightly sloping sides. This can be achieved by simply lining an excavation with hand-mixed, or ready-mixed, concrete and although it is the least technical option, it does present certain difficulties. Despite these, this is the technique I have chosen to use here.

Making a start

It is a good idea to buy the paving before you start so that you can place it out on the ground, allowing for eventual mortar joints, and mark out the *inside* edge of the pool. At this point you will have to work out how far back from this line you will need to dig in order to fit an appropriate thickness of concrete. The concrete will be about 125mm (5in) thick, on top of which will be about 15mm (¾in) of rendering – if you are building in heavy clay, you need to make the concrete thicker. In

This pool has had an extra pair of slabs incorporated at each end to give it extra length and therefore different proportions

> **As a formal pool, it must sit comfortably within a reasonably large open space and, if possible, line up with a view or vista from the house** "

This formal layout, complete with box and lavender hedges, has been designed around its formal pool and fountain

This pool is based on a 2.7m (9ft) diameter 'stone' circle kit but could just as easily be based on one a little smaller, using only two rows of circles – one for the ends, the other for the sides

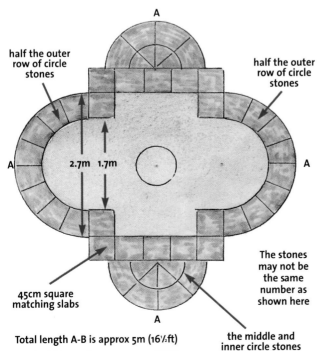

half the outer row of circle stones

half the outer row of circle stones

A

A

A

A

2.7m 1.7m

45cm square matching slabs

The stones may not be the same number as shown here

the middle and inner circle stones (half on each side)

Total length A-B is approx 5m (16½ft)

Total width C-D is approx 5.4m (18ft)

addition, the sides should, when finished, be set back under the paving by about 15mm to create an overhang. Altogether this means excavating back by about 155mm (6in). Shelves will be needed for planting and the pool should be at least 60cm (24in) deep. As well as the sides, the base will also have to be dug out 155mm deeper than the finished level.

Using pegs

Pegs can be useful for guiding your work – you could set several pegs around the edge of the excavation so that their tops indicate the level you need to dig to if the concrete is to finish up at exactly the right level. In this instance, there must be room to mortar the coping stones on top of the concrete while at the same time ensuring that they end up *just* below the level of the lawn for easy mowing. Once concrete covers the surface of the excavation, it is impossible to tell how thick it is.

Thin pegs can be pushed into the surface of the excavation and marked to show how thick the concrete must be. By making these pegs longer than is necessary, you will be able to take

hold of the portion still protruding from the finished concrete and pull them out as soon as concreting is complete. It is most important to slope the sides of the excavation since it will prove impossible to stack the concrete against vertical sides.

Placing

A mix, using 1 part cement to 6 parts of all-in ballast must have only just enough water added to create very stiff, yet thoroughly wetted, concrete. If it is too wet and sloppy, it will all end up in the bottom of the excavation!

About half the concrete is laid throughout the excavation before steel rods, thin enough to bend, are placed on top. An alternative to rods is a thick steel mesh or netting but it must be flexible enough to cope with the awkward shape. The final layer of concrete is then added and 'tamped', or banged down, using a block of wood to compact it.

By now, the concrete should be up to all the marks on the thin pegs and at the correct level around the top. As

you finish off, pull out all the thin pegs and put in a small overflow pipe right at the top together with another short length of pipe to take the electricity cable. The concrete must be covered with polythene and be left to set for a couple of days.

Rendering

Left as it is, the concrete will not be watertight so it must be rendered. This means using a mix in the proportion of 1 part of cement to 5 parts of sharp sand with enough water to give it a 'pasty' consistency. The easiest way to apply it is with the head of an old soft broom, brushing it on about 1cm (½in) thick. Once this has set under polythene for a day or two, a further layer can be brushed on. When this layer has also set, it should be completely watertight but it could have either a waterproofing

agent added to it during mixing, or be painted over with a suitable water-proofing 'paint' which will come with very specific instructions that must be followed carefully. GRP (see page 90) gives even better protection.

If all your preparation has been carried out carefully, the pond should now be just the right size and shape to sit comfortably under the coping stone with a small overhang.

Fountain choice

The most important point in choosing a fountain is to make sure that it is not so vigorous that, on a windy day, it blows all over the surrounding paving and lawn, and therefore loses valuable water.

The cable will need hiding as will a suitable outdoor electrical socket. This is not always easy to achieve with a formal pond. It can be helpful to buy a pump which has a long cable that can go in ducting under the lawn and reach a socket hidden in some nearby planting.

Preparing for pond-life

Whichever method of waterproofing you have used, the pond must be thoroughly rinsed. This is usually done by filling and emptying it several times. There should be several shelves on which baskets of marginal and aquatic plants can go, perhaps with a water lily growing in a basket on the floor of the pond. Water lilies are useful if fish are to be added because the leaves give them some protection from herons while some Canadian pond weed – *Elodia canadensis* – will help to increase oxygen levels.

There are some in-pond filter systems available if you want crystal clear water but these may require small modifications to the pond shape at the outset if they are to be incorporated successfully.

Choose from several effective recipes for building a raised pool

Taking an elevated

Raising a pond can make it just that little bit more special than having it flush with the ground. Patio pools are often raised so you can sit on the edge and appreciate the pond life at closer quarters.

It may also be the only way of having a pond if, for some reason, it cannot be dug into the ground. If a very deep pond is needed, then elevating it would mean less excavation.

Raised ponds, built all on

their own out in the middle of a garden can, however, look rather ungainly. They may look better as part of a dedicated area with paths, seating and associated borders.

A raised pond can be a disincentive to herons, and provide an easier way of hiding a filtration system.

There are, of course, many ways of building a raised pond, but bear in mind that because it will be under close scrutiny it

will need especially careful construction.

A raised pond can be virtually any shape, but a square pool within curved surroundings can look awkward and vice versa.

The usual rules about positioning still apply – some sun but perhaps not all day long, not immediately beneath large trees and not too far from a power supply if a pump, lighting or winter heater are likely to be used – raised ponds can be par-

ticularly vulnerable to freezing.

The water can be contained in a pre-moulded tank or fibreglass mould, a liner – butyl or something similar or in a construction using concrete, stone and other 'hard' materials.

Pre-formed tanks

The easiest option is a pre-moulded shape, preferably in fibreglass rather than plastic. Apart from all the free-form

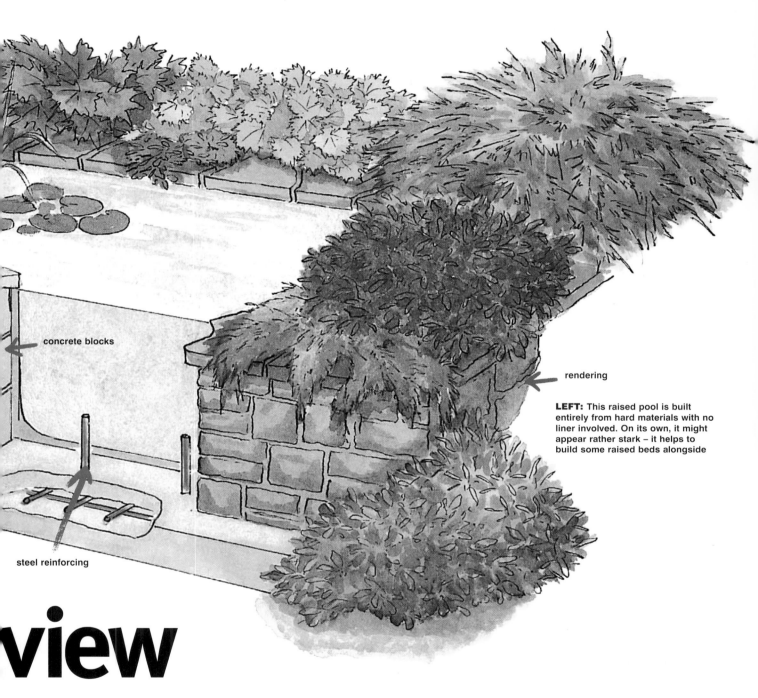

concrete blocks

rendering

LEFT: This raised pool is built entirely from hard materials with no liner involved. On its own, it might appear rather stark – it helps to build some raised beds alongside

steel reinforcing

view

ponds available, there are also various geometric or formal shapes.

Depth is important since anything too shallow might freeze. Ideally, a raised pond should never be less than 35cm (14in) deep except perhaps in a city where it could be a little less.

In general terms, a tank or moulded pool is reasonably self-supporting, so should not require a particularly strong structure around it, whereas liners have no

strength and therefore have to rely entirely on the structure around them for support.

A liner is almost certainly going to be in contact with some rough surfaces, so it must be used in conjunction with a good underfelt – probably several thicknesses of it in places.

A rigid pool made entirely from 'hard' materials may not naturally be watertight. It will usually need some form of water-proofing treatment on the

inside and, unlike the other types of pool, a 'hard' structure cannot give under duress so must be extra strong.

'Hard' materials

This is the most involved option but, until liners were widely available, used to be the most common technique.

A concrete base is created either on or in the ground about 10cm (4in) bigger all round than the finished pool and at

least 15cm (6in) thick.

The concrete mix might be one part of cement to six parts of 'all-in ballast' plus, of course, sufficient water to produce a fairly stiff mix – not so runny as to pour.

Some steel – preferably steel grid – should be incorporated more or less through the centre, which means laying about half the concrete, placing the steel and then laying the rest on top.

Some 'L'-shaped lengths of

ABOVE: The formality of this square brick pond edged with stone is softened by the plantings

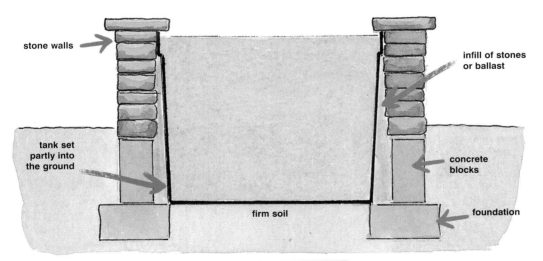

stone walls

infill of stones
or ballast

tank set
partly into
the ground

concrete
blocks

firm soil

foundation

DESIGN AND PLANTING HINTS

RAISED PONDS, like any others, will support all sorts of pond life, but the fact that the pond is raised may well exclude frogs, toads and perhaps newts, unless some sort of ramp is provided at critical times of the year.

Relatively few aquatic or marginal plants have a trailing habit but those which do – including *Ajuga reptans* and *Lysimachia nummularia* – can be planted as closely as possible to the edges of plant baskets and encouraged to come over the sides of the pond.

Better still, raised beds could join the elevated pond and provide the opportunity for a much wider range of trailing plants to grow down over the edges.

Pots of plants clustered at various points around the pond will also help to soften the walls and integrate the structure into its surroundings.

steel are needed all around the edge so that they protrude from the raft of concrete precisely along the centre of what will be a double-skin pool wall.

The walls can then be built up either side of these vertical pieces of steel, the outer skin being in the chosen material – stock bricks, stone etc. – and the inner skin something less expensive like 10cm (4in) thick concrete blocks.

These walls will, of course, be mortared together and the small space between the two can be

packed with the same mortar.

The use of concrete allows virtually any pool shape, as concrete blocks for the inner skin can be cut and broken as often as necessary, these being eventually covered over with rendering.

Rendering

Once the walls are up to the right height, the coping can be mortared on. This should overhang the outside by about 2cm (¾in), and about 3cm (1¼in) on the inside, so as to allow for the rendering.

At the same time, an overflow and maybe a cable entry point can be created.

Rendering is a pasty mix of one part cement, six parts of sharp sand, water and a waterproofing agent.

The mix can be brushed on in two layers, a few hours apart, using the head of an old, fairly stiff, yard broom. The amount of water must be just right.

The aim is to cover the inside of the whole structure thoroughly and to taper the render

"Depth is important since anything too shallow might freeze"

slightly so that it is a little thinner towards the top.

The finished surface is lightly textured and stone-coloured.

Importantly, the concrete, mortar and rendered surface must be kept covered with a PVC sheet so that it can cure properly without drying out or freezing. Once set, the rendered surface could be painted with an additional waterproofing agent which will also ensure that no free lime raises the pH of the water too high for healthy pond life. GRP (see page 90) is an alternative worth considering. Only when the pond is complete should shelves or plinths be added for baskets of aquatic and marginal plants.

Brick/stone with liner
Instead of a solid raft of concrete, the base of the pond can be of compacted soil or an existing paved surface, possibly with a layer of sand over the top.

The walls must, however, be given a proper concrete foundation, but just a strip all round, twice the width of the wall.

Existing paving may well suffice for a foundation if it appears to be sound and stable, but paving is often laid to a fall and the pond must be dead level, so some adjustments may be necessary within the mortar joints.

It is important to remember that the liner will depend upon these walls for support, so they must be as strong as those described for the 'hard' structure above.

There are two major problems with a liner: it is prone to puncture and is visually ugly, especially when the water level begins to drop through evaporation.

This can largely be overcome by running the liner up behind several courses of brick or stone laid to finish off the inside walls, but it will need extra protection from rough surfaces.

These last few 'ornamental' courses must not be mortared on top of the liner until the pond has been filled up to this point with water and the liner allowed to settle and stretch for several hours.

As before, an overflow, a cable

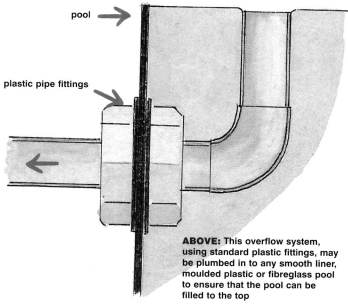

pool

plastic pipe fittings

ABOVE: This overflow system, using standard plastic fittings, may be plumbed in to any smooth liner, moulded plastic or fibreglass pool to ensure that the pool can be filled to the top

entry point and a coping are needed.

Timber with liner
This is probably the easiest option because it does not require an elaborate foundation. It must, however, be perfectly level and the timbers must be substantial.

Real railway sleepers could be used, but they do exude tar in hot weather, which may rule

out sitting on the edge of the pool unless a separate timber coping is used.

You could try using Forest Fencing Mini Sleepers which do not exude tar and are easier to handle.

Timbers are usually laid horizontally as for a log cabin, and nailed, screwed, bolted or notched to lock together.

Traditionally, the liner is run up and over the last but one sleeper.

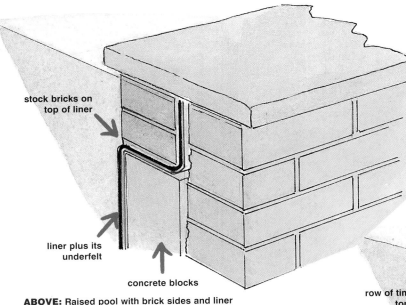

stock bricks on
top of liner

liner plus its
underfelt

concrete blocks

ABOVE: Raised pool with brick sides and liner

"Only when the pond is complete should shelves or plinths be added for baskets of aquatic and marginal plants"

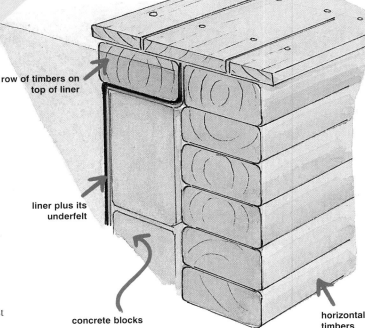

BELOW: Timber raised pool with liner

coping

row of timbers on
top of liner

liner plus its
underfelt

concrete blocks

horizontal
timbers

The top sleeper is then fixed down on top to clamp and secure the liner, the problem being that the liner can be seen when the water begins to evaporate.

An alternative approach is to build up a wall of 10cm- (4in) thick concrete blocks on the inside of the timber walls until they are precisely one sleeper down from the top – it may be necessary to finish off with some odd materials to achieve this.

Using the same idea as in the previous construction, the liner is brought up and over the top of this wall before finally going vertical again up the back of the top sleeper.

A second top sleeper is then laid on top of the liner parallel to the other one and a wooden coping, easily wide enough to cover both, is fixed down to secure the row of inner sleepers.

With the liner coming vertically right up to the underside of the coping, the pond can fill right up and would have to drop the thickness of one sleeper before the liner became visible.

It is possible that the pressure treatment used in the sleepers could escape into the water from this extra row of internal timbers. Oak or chestnut timbers – which are unlikely to have been treated by anything – may be used instead.

As with the previous structure, the pond must be filled up to this crossover point and the liner stretched before the internal sleepers are put in place. Most timber ponds have to be geometric in shape, including hexagons, octagons and so on.

It cannot be overstated that liners must be adequately cushioned from scuffing and sharp corners.

Pre-formed moulds

While walls need not be as robust as those described for the previous structures, it is vitally important that the moulded shape sits firmly on or in the ground.

This is easy to achieve with a symmetrical shape like a circle or a rectangle, but much more difficult with an asymmetrical free-form moulded fibreglass pool which may require some packing out to prevent it tilting once filled with water.

When stability is assured, walls of the chosen material can be built up around the outside. Again, with free-form shapes there will be large voids in places between the vertical walls and the shaped side of the moulded pool.

Ideally these should be packed with either soil or stones.

The mould will be visible when the water level drops but, on the whole, fibreglass or plastic is not quite as ugly as a liner.

ABOVE: Bricks form the lip of this circular pool fringed with flowers and seen at the 1999 Tatton Flower Show

Raising your standards

Add interest and height to your garden by making a raised pond

Any raised feature in an otherwise flat garden will help to add interest, but one containing water is always special.

To make this kind of feature look attractive you will need to put thought into its planning and leave plenty of room for planting. The drawings on the next three pages show an idea which is relatively easy to construct, not especially expensive, and which is almost like a miniature garden. It is built around three pools, two of which have some movement of water between them, and is on four different levels with a fair amount of space for planting.

Size

The size of the water feature is governed by the diameter of the three pools, all of which are circular domestic water storage tanks. The top one has a diameter of about 70cm (27in) and the other two, diameters of 85cm (33in) – but larger tanks, and pre-formed

ABOVE: A raised pool can add another dimension to the garden

round pools, are available.

Based on these sizes, this particular project covers an area about 2.6m (8ft 6in) by 3m (10ft). The highest part is about 90cm (3ft) above ground level and the lowest, 15cm (6in).

Siting

You will need an open and fairly sunny site well away from overhanging trees and with some form of access on at least two sides. It should not be built on weed infested or sloping ground nor be so far away from the house that it is 'lost in the wilderness'. Close to a patio or garden seating area is ideal so that you can sit and watch the pond life and hear the moving water.

Starting

The ground must be levelled and cleared of all weed. Setting out shapes is the first job and since the whole project is centred around the pools, the position and size of these must be marked clearly and accurately on the ground. A white aerosol paint is an effective way of 'drawing' on firm soil. Next, the circular log walls are plotted but it may take several attempts to

get these exactly right. Note that not all the pools are positioned centrally within a 'circular' bed.

Building walls

Log poles and sleepers are usually concreted into a narrow trench. If the poles have an average diameter of 75mm (3in) the trench will be about 25cm (10in) wide. Ideally, poles for the tallest bed, at 90cm (35in), should have about half their length under ground – about 40 to 45cm (15 to 17in) although

you might get away with less than this for the lower beds.

Set each pole dead vertical with a spirit level and make sure they follow a good smooth curve with no 'flat' sections. Treat any cut surfaces with extra preservative before immersing them in concrete.

Concrete, which should be mixed 'stiff' rather than runny, is packed down hard on either side of the poles and left to set before any more work is carried out.

> "Perhaps the most important thing to bear in mind is that plants should not be so tall as to hide the various levels"

Top pool

The tank will have to be set carefully onto the concrete blocks at a height where its rim is about 10mm (1/2in) below the top of the wall. Make sure the concrete blocks are set firmly into the ground, and protect the bottom of the tank by placing a piece of geotextile matting or roofing felt between it and the blocks. Once the tank has been plumbed in, filled and packed around with soil, it shouldn't move.

Plumbing

Before packing any soil around the top tank, plumb in a length of plastic overflow pipe, using the appropriate fittings from a plumber's merchant, on the side which faces the next pool down.

Fig 1 Three raised pools with two linked and four levels

Fig 2 The tanks before planting

It probably will not need to be much more than about 30cm (12in) long – enough to go from inside the tank through to the outside of the log wall. Left like this, the pipe would look ugly so it will have to go inside a bamboo 'sleeve'. This is a length of bamboo pipe at least 25mm (1in) in diameter which will be fixed into the log wall, protrude at the front by about 10cm (4in) and slope down slightly. The end hanging out over the lower pool must be given a slanting cut so that water is thrown clear. The hole that you drill or cut through the log wall must therefore be large enough to take the bamboo pipe even though this does not go into the tank itself. The plastic pipe goes well into the bamboo pipe but stops short of the front

so that it is not visible.

Although the bamboo pipe slopes down slightly and water is therefore unlikely to leak backwards when it comes out of the plastic pipe, it is a good idea to seal up the gap between the two, from behind, with a water-

tight mastic. Water will then be able to flow cleanly and safely from the upper pool down into the one below.

Smaller pools

The other two pools can now be installed. It is unlikely that they

will need to go on blocks. One will probably be set into the ground and the other, sit on it. The pool into which the water flows houses a submersible pump. From this will come a flexible hose which must pass invisibly to the upper pool. You

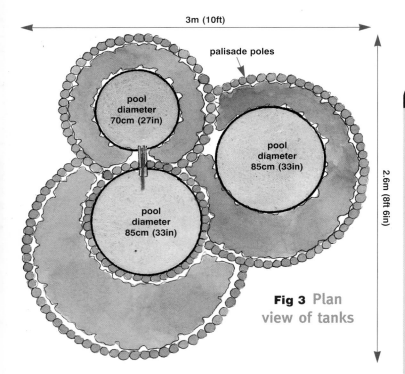

3m (10ft)

palisade poles

pool diameter 70cm (27in)

pool diameter 85cm (33in)

pool diameter 85cm (33in)

2.6m (8ft 6in)

Fig 3 Plan view of tanks

MATERIALS

Apart from the pre-formed pools, this project will use a considerable number of palisade poles which will have to be various lengths in order to create the different walls. These will be set into concrete which will require a quantity of all-in ballast and cement. The highest pool is supported on a number of concrete blocks and a quantity of topsoil will be needed to fill up the various planting spaces.

The moving water will flow through a length of plastic overflow pipe, together with suitable plumbing fittings, as well as through a short length of bamboo pipe with a diameter of at least 25mm (1in).

You will also need a small quantity of geotextile matting or roofing felt to go under the top pool and possibly some polythene if you decide to turn one of the lower beds into a boggy area. A submersible pump is needed along with some flexible hose to reach from the lower pool into the top one, and a safe outdoor electrical supply, fitted by a qualified electrician.

Although the log poles are already pressure-treated against decay, it would be wise to have some extra colourless preservative to treat any cut ends – and if you choose to change the colour of the log poles, you will need a suitable wood stain.

will have to decide how best to hide this, and the electric cable, before packing topsoil tightly around all three pools.

Warning: Do not let the end of the flexible hose go beneath the surface of the water in the top pool. If it does, then water will be siphoned out every time the pump is switched off. This siphoning continues until water in the top pool drops and no longer reaches the end of the hose.

Planting

Perhaps the most important thing to bear in mind is that plants should not be so tall as to

BOGGY OPTION

The largest lower bed which goes part way around the lower pool could be partially lined with black PVC so that the soil remains fairly boggy and can therefore support a range of moisture-loving plants.

Placed into an excavation about 45cm (18in) deep, without drain holes, the PVC comes up to within about 15cm (6in) of the surface so that only the lower part of the bed is waterlogged.

hide the various levels. In this example I have used some moisture-loving plants in the lowest beds but kept the height down immediately in front of the adjacent pool. Plants here include small hostas, water forget-me-not, lamium, and, towards the back where height is not so critical, *Lobelia cardinalis* and *Arundinaria fortunei*. The other low bed has pansies, hakonechloa, liriope, and *Iris pallida* 'Variegata'. At the top is a small weeping conifer, a prostrate cotoneaster, genista and *Festuca glauca*.

None of these plants is especially pH sensitive but if you wanted to grow some ericaceous plants – such as heathers and dwarf rhododendrons – you would have to ensure that your imported topsoil was acid, with a low pH.

In the ground around the outside edge are various small plants growing between the stones. These include *Viola labradorica*, more pansies, and another hakonechloa. To make one level flow visually into the next, some plants can be

repeated so that they appear to spill down onto the next layer.

It is important to include some evergreens since a feature like this will probably be sited somewhere that is highly visible all year round. The pools themselves could have baskets of aquatic and marginal plants

with the baskets being set at different depths, perhaps with the use of concrete blocks or bricks, to suit the plants growing in them. One of the pools has no water movement and will therefore benefit from some oxygenating weed such as *Elodea canadensis*.

Fig 4

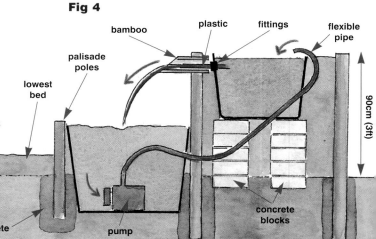

bamboo

plastic

fittings

flexible pipe

palisade poles

lowest bed

90cm (3ft)

concrete

pump

concrete blocks

GARDEN THEMES & FEATURES

HARRY SMITH COLLECTION

Getting to the bottom of it

"The effects a cascade can give range from a mountain stream with a series of falls, to a single cascade pouring from a vertical rock face"

LEFT: Excitement in plenty from this dramatic cascade

be used to modernistic effect.

Construction pitfalls concern the fact that all these projects rely on recycling the same water; if any of this water escapes, the cascade soon appears empty, so attention to detail is essential.

Artificial cascades

Moulded 'rocky' sections which fit together as a kit to form a series of cascades are available at most large garden centres. You may feel these hardly qualify as DIY cascades, but you will still have to spend time on peripheral work if these are to look authentic.

The most realistic moulded cascades are made from thin, lightweight concrete, and perhaps the least convincing are those made from shiny plastic. Because a series of cascades can lose a fair amount of water through evaporation, they must ultimately flow into a generous pond or reservoir at the bottom.

This is where a submersible pump operates – taking water and pushing it up through a hidden pipe to the highest cascade. If the cascades have partly dried up through lack of use, it could take a considerable volume of water from the bottom pond to top them all up to overflowing.

The bottom pond should, therefore, be designed to provide this initial volume of water

without looking too depleted. Most of these moulded cascades must be fitted into a slope, so that water from one can flow down into the next.

Each section must be set perfectly level so that it remains full of water when the pump is switched off. To make these sections look as natural as possible, additional rock can be laid in terraces on either side, thus making the cascades look as if they are part of more extensive rocky terraces.

The point at which the delivery pipe enters the top cascade must be carefully disguised, as must other pipework and cables. Planting with low-spreading shrubby plants – including small conifers – usually looks more impressive than annual flowers.

This perennial planting can be useful to disguise any obvious joints and will remain in place both summer and winter. Additional rock work and careful planting can go a long way to make these artificial cascades look natural.

The effects a cascade can give range from a mountain stream with a series of falls to a single cascade pouring from a vertical rock face. It might be a grotto with water cascading down from the roof, or a curtain of water pouring almost silently from a stone wall.

All these ideas will depend

The key to making successful cascades

Even in a small space, a cascade can be a beautiful addition to your garden, allowing water to flow or tumble from one level to another – either in a relatively gentle fashion or, more dramatically and noisily, from a high point.

Most cascades are modelled along natural lines, but wooden channels and sheets of glass can

"Additional rock work and careful planting can go a long way to make these artificial cascades look natural"

LEFT: Low-spreading hosta enhances this creation

trees where falling leaves could foul up the whole system.

When using rockery stone, bear in mind that good-sized squarish chunks will be much easier to work with than smaller random-shaped pieces.

An overall shell of concrete could be used to contain the water, but it must be reinforced with steel and rendered to make it waterproof. Rocks can be easily mortared into position for the creation of fairly watertight falls.

A butyl liner is easier to handle, but rocks could cause damage if it isn't bedded onto an underfelt and covered with a PVC sheet together with a thick layer of mortar. It may also be more difficult to create completely watertight falls.

To elevate the project on a flat

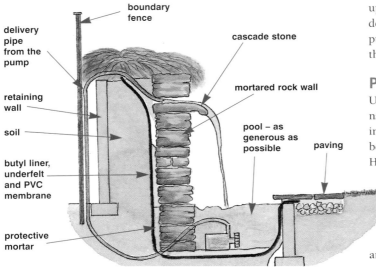

boundary fence

delivery pipe from the pump

cascade stone

retaining wall

mortared rock wall

soil

pool – as generous as possible

paving

butyl liner, underfelt and PVC membrane

protective mortar

ABOVE: The liner must isolate the wet soil and rocks from surrounding materials in the actual cascade

upon the right flow of water, delivered by an appropriate pump situated in a reservoir at the bottom of the feature.

Position

Unless the garden is on a natural slope, it is almost inevitable that the setting will be anything but natural. However, some situations should always be avoided: don't have a cascade appearing to come directly out from a garden fence or garage wall, and don't place one under large

RIGHT: This dramatic corner cascade is only about 4ft 6in or 5ft high (1.5m). It is backed by a retaining wall and water flows vigorously from a crevice in the rock face down into a rock pool. A liner is used to contain the complete water course

ABOVE: This rockery by Douglas Knight at the 1999 Tatton Park Show is natural and informal

site, retaining walls, walls of rock, timber walls and blanks are all options depending upon the type of project and cost.

Vertical cascade

This feature is ideal for a corner with a fence or wall behind. Space must be left for some background planting like climbers. Butyl can be made to work quite well here but extra care must be taken to ensure that the considerable weight of stone does not cause any damage.

A generous pool or reservoir is essential because a vigorous flow can sometimes hit rocks and splash out of the system altogether. Construction resembles a tall but fairly narrow raised bed.

The back wall can be in concrete blocks but elsewhere the walls will have to be made from rockery stones mortared together. Water is quite simply pumped from the pool to a hole in the rocks near the top.

Ideally, the water should flow out over a flattish stone which is shaped (throated) so that water can flow off in a 'curtain' rather than dribble back down the rock face. The liner must have an underfelt and be covered with a PVC sheet before a generous layer of soft sand mortar is placed on top.

It can be assumed that all the rocks which go down into the pool as well as those beneath and on either side of the cascade will be constantly wet. The liner must therefore follow behind – and between – all the way to the top ensuring that all this dampness is kept separated from the relatively dry stones and soil around.

The liner will need some

DIY CASCADE

A DIY cascade is a much greater challenge than an artificial creation, because how the water is conducted and retained must be considered along with the overall appearance.

Key considerations are:
● What type of effect do you want to create?
● Where in the garden will it be positioned?
● What materials should be used?
● How can the area be elevated – if it isn't already on a slope?

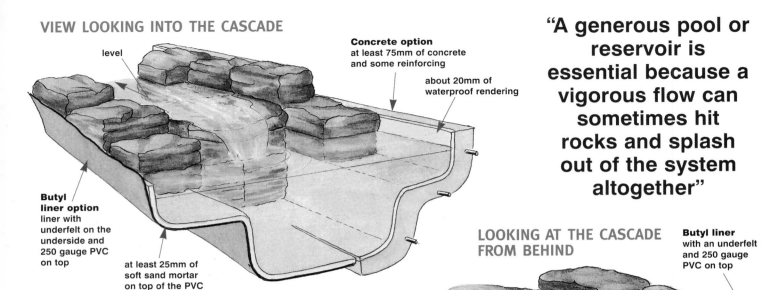

VIEW LOOKING INTO THE CASCADE

level

Concrete option
at least 75mm of concrete and some reinforcing

about 20mm of waterproof rendering

"A generous pool or reservoir is essential because a vigorous flow can sometimes hit rocks and splash out of the system altogether"

Butyl liner option
liner with underfelt on the underside and 250 gauge PVC on top

at least 25mm of soft sand mortar on top of the PVC

LOOKING AT THE CASCADE FROM BEHIND

Butyl liner
with an underfelt and 250 gauge PVC on top

Concrete option
at least 75mm of concrete and some reinforcing

about 20mm of waterproof render-ing taken right up and under the waterfall stone

Using a liner

each section is level

mortar/rendering

at least 25mm o soft san and mortar

mortar or render-ing goes right up into here and under the waterfall stone

possible support walls

very careful positioning and perhaps disguising. The pump will have to be reasonably powerful to lift the water and provide a good fall; some stones may need adjusting or adding to prevent water from splashing out of the pool.

Potential damage to the liner, creeping dampness and splash-ing are the main points to watch out for. The more soil pockets there are for planting, the better.

The illustration shows mostly perennial planting, such as shrubs and ferns which give a fairly green and permanent effect, with climbers hiding the fence behind. Eventually the rocks will become mossy and discoloured, producing a cave-like effect. This type of feature could be quite noisy, so do consider your neighbours!

Mountain stream

Doing-it-yourself rather than from kits offers more challenge, see panel, and even more exacting – and requiring more space – is building a mountain stream.

If the garden is flat, then a way must be found of raising part of it, perhaps by using low walls or banks – not as an island in the centre of the garden but perhaps to one side where it could be imagined that the ground in a neighbouring property is also elevated.

It is important to compact thoroughly any raised ground

along the route of the stream and cascades so that it does not subside over the years – especial-ly so if concrete is involved.

If a liner is used, then ideally this should be continuous throughout the cascade with a generous overlap onto the main pool liner. Where several cascades are planned, it will be more interesting to have them at different heights – and possibly angles.

Work starts with the main pool which could be rock lined to match the cascades.

Any butyl not disguised by rocks can be hidden by a layer of mortar. The first cascade or waterfall may be created on a shelf within the pool so that there is a

generous overlap of liners.

To make sure concrete does not crack around any of the cascades, incorporate plenty of reinforcing material. In both the butyl and concrete projects, the whole system is first built as an empty stepped stream with no rocks.

The concrete must be rendered and the butyl coated with mortar before rocks are added to any shelves and built across, like a dam, to create the falls or cascades. The overall affect will be improved if, as with the artificial cascades, further rocks are arranged in terraces on either side.

During construction, a pipe

and cable must be incorporated. As soil is brought up around the edges ready for planting it is vital to ensure that none of the relatively dry garden soil or materials come into contact with the wet materials lining the cascades.

It is equally important to check that water is not splash-ing out of the system because of awkwardly shaped or positioned rocks.

As with previous projects, planting is important, so a good proportion of permanent shrubby plants should be used along with some areas of seasonal or alpine colour.

Superb old wall-mounted fountain at Hestercombe gardens in Somerset – wall fountains are not always as simple as they appear but are worth the effort involved

Backs to the wall

Wall-mounted water features can give a garden an authentic Italian feel – and are great for small spaces

W ater features that go
on walls are always
appealing because
they make good use of space
and are ideal in tiny gardens and
courtyards. They are available in
a variety of attractive designs
and usually produce that lovely
trickling sound which is both
soothing and cooling rather than
intrusive. Unfortunately some
require a lot more installation
than meets the eye, and others

are inherently unreliable, so it
does pay to take a close look at
what is on offer and how they
compare on installation and
reliability.

Whose wall?
Most wall features need an
electricity supply and some
pipe-work, quite apart from
having to be fixed to the wall, so
if the wall is somebody else's,

you should ask permis-
sion before drilling holes in it.
This could restrict your choice
of feature or mean that you are
going to have to be cunning
when it comes to hiding pipes
and cables.

Wall suitability
Some wall features have to be
incorporated as the wall is being
built, or require part of an
existing wall to be demolished
so that it can be re-built around
the feature. Others are much less
disruptive and merely hang on
the wall. The wall can be in sun
or shade, but the sunnier the
wall the greater the risk of the
feature going green with algae.

However, there are various
additives which can be used to
reduce this problem.

Most of these features are small
and intimate, so a wall within a
yard or patio area will be more
effective than a more isolated one
further out in the garden.

Lion's head or mask
Some lion's heads or masks are
made from stone or concrete
and are therefore quite bulky.
They have to be fitted right into
the wall, which can be disruptive. It might sometimes be
appropriate to build up a false
wall in front of an existing one
or to replace part of a fence with

"Some of the most effective plants for this situation are perennial grasses and small bamboos together with some trailing or creeping plants"

ED GABRIEL

LEFT: Fig 1
Water from this cascade follows a tapered sheet of clear acrylic down into the pool and is therefore unlikely to touch the wall and be lost from the system on its way down

ABOVE: A dramatic effect can be achieved through simple means as in this garden by Butler Landscapes who exhibited at Tatton park in 1999

"Some wall features have to be incorporated as the wall is being built or require part of an existing wall to be demolished so that it can be re-built around the feature"

a section of wall just for the water feature. The moulded fibreglass features simply fix to the face of an existing wall but may not look quite so convincing.

A pipe which goes from the back of a 'solid' head into the mouth will have to be connected to a pump positioned in the pool or reservoir below – there is a similar arrangement for the 'hollow' features. This connecting pipe could go right through and behind the wall, or alternatively, up the face of it, but in this case it might not always be easy to disguise.

Some of these heads or masks may not throw their jet of water very far and on a windy day much of it could be blown off course and lost, so the pool below must be large enough to

take this into account. The pool will also need to be reasonably deep to accommodate the pump and not run dry through evaporation.

Another problem which can occur on windy days or when a partially blocked pump produces a dribble rather than a flow from the mouth is that water may splash, or dribble, onto the wall. This can then be lost through absorption into the brick or stone-work. A thorough coat of transparent resin, or silicone, on that part of the wall most affected will help to prevent this absorption and thus return most of the water to the pool. Very rustic walls may prove impossible to waterproof. The other likely bonus from treating the wall with resin or silicone is that algae are much less likely to form and discolour it.

DIY wall cascade

Fig 1 shows an idea which should at least partly overcome some of these problems, and is something which you might be able to make or adapt yourself, based on an existing wall. A tray made from a sheet of lead or aluminium has been made to fit in a gap between stones near the top of a wall. The tray would not be wider than about 15cm (6in) but could be as much as 5cm (2in) deep and certainly long enough to reach from front to back. Along its front edge is a lip which is bent vertically down by about 1cm (⅜in). At the back, a piece of rigid piping enters the tray and bends to deflect water down onto the floor of the tray. If it wasn't bent, the water would shoot straight out!

A length of flexible pipe is usually used to join the section

of rigid pipe with the pump which is in the reservoir below. This reservoir or pool utilises a preformed tank approximately 75cm (30in) across and 40cm (16in) deep. It sits within a stone wall which becomes a raised bed once soil has been added. If left like this, the feature would almost certainly lose water to the main wall because the cascade passes so close to it, so a sheet of clear acrylic has been fixed between the lip of the tray and the bottom of the pool to guide water down without any splashing.

Before this sheet can be fixed permanently, it is essential to get the water flowing into the tray as evenly as possible – the tray will need setting on some mortar to make sure it is dead flat, or possibly even tilting back a tiny amount – so that you can see the shape of the flow. Hopefully, it will emerge from the tray its full width, but it will then narrow as it falls into the pool. The acrylic sheet will have to be the same width as the tray at the top but

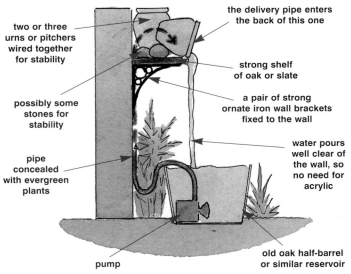

Fig 3 An idea which could be installed without drilling right through the wall

two or three urns or pitchers wired together for stability

the delivery pipe enters the back of this one

possibly some stones for stability

strong shelf of oak or slate

a pair of strong ornate iron wall brackets fixed to the wall

pipe concealed with evergreen plants

water pours well clear of the wall, so no need for acrylic

pump

old oak half-barrel or similar reservoir

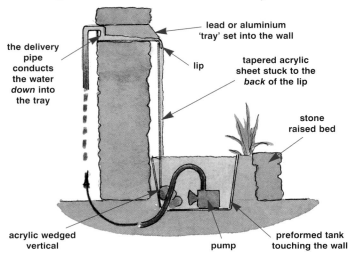

Fig 4 The wall cascade with acrylic 'fall'

lead or aluminium 'tray' set into the wall

the delivery pipe conducts the water *down* into the tray

lip

tapered acrylic sheet stuck to the *back* of the lip

stone raised bed

acrylic wedged vertical

pump

preformed tank touching the wall

must be cut and tapered to catch the flow of water. This will ensure that when the water is flowing, the acrylic is completely covered and therefore invisible. The amount of taper will depend upon the size of the pump (not too large), how close the down-turned end of the delivery pipe is to the floor of the tray, how far back it is from the lip, and the height of

drop down into the pool.

Acrylic sheet can be bought at most large DIY stores and cut with a 'laminate' cutter. Once it has been cut to match the flow, it can be fixed behind the lip with some clear, exterior mastic and wedged underwater with some stones. It must be vertical and not twisted. Where wildlife is likely to live in the pond, an algaecide can be introduced to minimise the

problem of green algae but where no pond-life is wanted, a sterilising agent, such as Milton, could be added to the water. The acrylic sheet will need cleaning from time to time if it is to remain a successful illusion. With the water being guided down into the pool there is little danger of any water loss, except through evaporation, which is why the pool can be a simple pre-formed tank which has only to briefly touch the wall at the back.

The raised bed around this tank provides a good opportunity to grow some plants which will help to hide the pool edges, the cable and pipework. Some of the most effective plants for this situation are perennial grasses and small bamboos together with some trailing or creeping plants. In addition, the illustration shows a few primulas and an ajuga for some seasonal colour.

Self-contained features

There are many self-contained features available, rather like the spouting cherub in fig 2. They are easy to install because most come complete with their own little pump and built-in pipework. Many just simply 'hang' on a wall but there will be

an electricity cable to hide. The one illustrated here is not, as most people have them, high up on a wall, but lower down so that it can be part of a more significant feature with some stone and terracotta bowls of mainly seasonal flowers. On a patio this could all be at eye level when viewed from a deck chair.

Fig 3 shows an urn pouring water from a shelf down into a half-barrel and is not exactly self-contained but should be feasible without having to drill the wall, apart from fixing two brackets. Again, a cable and, in this case, a pipe will need hiding, but there is plenty of opportunity for some planting. The feature is certainly a possibility where the wall is someone else's – and the water is thrown well clear, so there shouldn't be any dampness.

"Most of these features are small and intimate, so a wall within a yard or patio area will be more effective than a more isolated one further out in the garden"

"Apart from adding interest, the water is likely to encourage birds to come and bathe"

Rock around the clock

Creating a rock garden from scratch

ABOVE: Careful planting can create both height and fullness to a rock garden

Traditionally, rock gardens are planted with alpines, dwarf shrubs and miniature conifers, so the general idea is to try and reproduce part of a rocky hillside with terraces, ravines and perhaps some running water. Too often the rock garden has ended up as a pile of earth with stones and rocks stuffed randomly into it!

Siting

Ideally, of course, a rock garden would be best built into a natural slope or bank, but that is not always possible. The type of plants usually grown in rock gardens grow best in an open, perhaps sunny position well away from overhanging trees – one of the worst places would be against the trunk of a large tree.

If a natural bank is used, but it slopes away from the house, you could put a seat opposite so that the rocky terraces and planting can be appreciated.

Perennial weeds are the

"...the general idea is to try and reproduce part of a rocky hillside with terraces, ravines and perhaps some running water"

biggest scourge, coming up between heavy rocks and through tiny plants to make weed control almost impossible, so a weed-free site is essential.

Heavy clay is not as suitable as a lighter well-drained soil. With so much tiny detail in a rock garden, it would be better close to the house or a patio than a great distance away.

Although it will be elevated, the rock garden should never be constructed in waterlogged ground – very few alpines could tolerate this, especially in winter.

Rocks

The overall appearance of a rock garden depends very much on the type of rock used. For example,

slate is usually quite flat so rocky terraces are likely to end up relatively flat and sprawling. Purbeck stone on the other hand often occurs in block-shaped pieces, making it quite easy to stack them on top of one another to

produce higher and more dramatic terraces.

Slate is usually grey, and Purbeck a creamy colour. There are obviously many different types of stone available but the cheapest are often those which come from a quarry closest to you since transportation can be very costly.

Having chosen a rock, it is then important to make sure that any paving, walling, steps, and gravel match.

Construction

Since construction will be largely in the form of ascending terraces, the first rocks to be placed are those at the very bottom and furthest forward, preferably not in a straight line but with some interesting 'ins and outs'. At the same

time, the lower portion of a retaining wall can be built up to a similar height and the space between filled with good well-drained, weed-free topsoil – preferably slightly alkaline. This must be well compacted before the next layer or terrace of rocks is built on top, stepped back a little and ideally tilting very gently backwards. This tilt will help to reduce the risk of soil erosion. It may be possible to incorporate some steps here and there and to create a sheer or vertical rock face using several rocks on top of one another.

Where a rock garden is being added to the edge of an existing pond, several large rocks could rise up out of the water and become part of the first terrace. It is all too easy to create just a series of straight terraces rather like huge steps so some imagi-

It is important to limit the number of tall plants – otherwise all the rocks would be hidden under a mound of vegetation

nation is needed to make sure that there are plenty of craggy, uneven outcrops where a selection of plants can spill over and out of interesting crevices.

Existing bank

If you are building into an existing bank the construction is much the same – without, of course, the retaining wall – but there will be a greater tendency to create boring, step-like terraces. One way of avoiding this is to re-sculpture the bank so that it has some dramatic ins and outs. It will also help to build the rocky outcrops at an angle to the bank rather than in straight parallel lines.

Scree area

Some alpines prefer to grow in a deep bed of scree – that is, broken or crushed rocks and gravel. This could be about

RIGHT: Choice of rock type will make a difference to the overall look and choice of plants

ANDREA HARGREAVES

The rock garden before planting

planting terraces, topped
with sterilized
soil/compost

dry stone
retaining wall
for planting

water cascading from
rocks into a pebbly pool

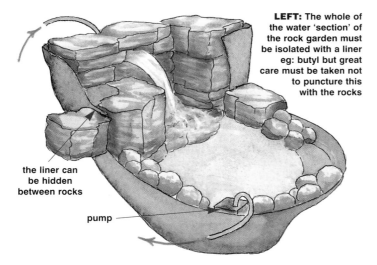

LEFT: The whole of
the water 'section' of
the rock garden must
be isolated with a liner
eg: butyl but great
care must be taken not
to puncture this
with the rocks

the liner can
be hidden
between rocks

pump

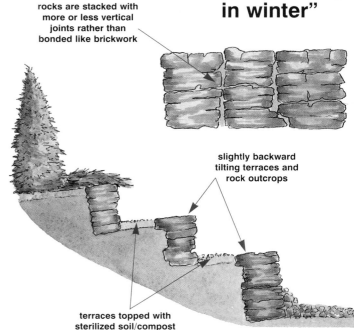

rocks are stacked with
more or less vertical
joints rather than
bonded like brickwork

slightly backward
tilting terraces and
rock outcrops

terraces topped with
sterilized soil/compost

10cm (4in) deep and perhaps at the foot of a crevice, stretching out across the lower part of the rock garden. Some of the plants here may need protecting with some glass in winter.

Sunken area

In well drained soils a rock-lined gully or gorge could be incorporated at the foot of the rock garden by excavating some soil. This soil can then be used, if it is suitable, elsewhere in the rock garden and it should be possible to create, at one end, an extra high rock face with the added depth. This sunken area

will probably always tend to be relatively damp and thus restrict the choice of plants.

A useful tip is to leave the level of topsoil in each planting area low, by about 25mm (1in) and then to top up with John Innes potting No 2. It is sterile so no weeds will grow for several weeks. Once the plants are in, each terrace can be dressed with an appropriate gravel.

Incorporating water

If the rock garden is to have its own water feature, then this must be planned at the outset since even the simplest ideas need very careful construction. It is vital that any part of the rock garden directly in contact with water is separated from the rest so that wet rocks and soil cannot transmit moisture to the drier parts and therefore lose water from the system. This is often best achieved with the discreet use of a butyl liner. A modest waterfall cascading into

a small rocky stream which then flows a short distance to a pool – the reservoir – is fairly easy to build within a liner, using mortar to fix rocks around the edges and a small submersible pump down in the pool. Apart from adding interest, the water is likely to encourage birds to come and bathe.

Planting

There is quite an art to planting a rock garden effectively and it all hinges on selecting plants of the right height and habit. Dwarf shrubs and upright conifers, for example, can be ideal for increasing the height of the highest outcrops while flat-tish plants go into the lower areas. This accentuates the high and low spots, giving the whole feature a more dramatic appear-

ance. Other small shrubs and conifers can be used elsewhere to create points of interest – miniature weeping trees can be very effective – but in the main it will be areas of alpines which grow only a few centimetres high that will dominate the terraces producing a patchwork of colour, mostly in the spring but at other times too. There are many miniature bulbs suitable for a rock garden and these will have to be planted beneath the carpet of alpines. Some alpines like it shady and damp, others prefer it hot and dry, but a well constructed rock garden should provide all these conditions and while most of the colour will come from flowers, there are plenty of alpines with attractively coloured foliage for year round interest.

MOVING ROCKS

One of the most effective ways of moving heavy rocks is to run them on planks and rollers. The rollers must be about 7.5cm (3in) in diameter especially if they are having to travel across a lawn.

Going caving

No 18th-century landscape garden was complete without one, and they made a comeback at the 2001 Chelsea and Hampton Court shows. Here's how to make... a cave or grotto

I magine what fun it would be to have your very own cave or grotto tucked away somewhere in the garden. It could even have water cascading from the top into a pool below. The cave shown here could be almost any size, and is not especially difficult to construct, although some of the rocks would be very heavy.

BELOW: In this design seen at Chelsea light falls on a pool within the cave

Location

Ideally, a cave should be set into a natural bank. If the bank is not very high the whole feature could be sunk into the ground a little way to give the cave entrance more height.

If there is no bank available, it could all be constructed against an old brick wall so long as rocks continued on

either side to make it look more convincing.

Building a free-standing cave on flat ground out in the open is the least convincing solution. A cave can look especially effective if it is hidden away so that you come upon it when walking through a relatively over-grown part of the garden, perhaps in a

ED GABRIEL

wooded area or a dense shrubbery.

Falling leaves can be a problem if the cave is over a pool, and this may need clearing out at least once a year, especially if fish are kept in the pool.

Rock type

Good-sized chunky pieces of rock are easier to build with rather than lots of small rounded pieces. The cave has to

be built up rather like a house, so the more block-shaped the rock the better.

Your cave will need a lintel stone. This must be strong enough comfortably to span the entrance. It will almost certainly be one of the heaviest stones, and should be hand picked from the supplier's yard or quarry.

Some people argue that you should use stone that is indigenous to your area, but I think that within the confines of a garden this is less important than using a stone you can work with.

Foundation

The cave and its pool must have a good foundation to ensure that the whole structure does not subside or crack, as it will be extremely heavy.

The cave shown here is set into a natural bank and also down into the ground by about 45cm (18in), so a good quantity of soil will have to be excavated; not much of this will be reused within this project.

The ideal way to create a foundation

is to build a steel-reinforced concrete shell within a large sheet of butyl or PVC. This will be under great pressure so it must be laid on top of soft sand and an underfelt.

Inside this, more thick PVC sheeting is needed for protection before at least 10cm (4in) of concrete, with steel reinforcing, is laid in the shape of a pool.

Beneath the actual cave, the pool could be as much as 60cm (24in) deep, becoming a little shallower towards the front edges. An extra plinth of concrete – or concrete blocks, or pieces of stone mortared into position – is needed on either side of the pool to coincide with stonework for the cave entrance.

With a continuous liner beneath all this concrete, rendering or extra waterproofing should not be necessary.

Planting and paths

A stony path will be useful if steps have been incorporated into the side of the cave, and a path to and from the cave will help to link it with the rest of the garden.

A feature like this lends itself to 'themed' planting. The illustration, for example, shows mainly ferns and evergreen shrubs used with mosses to produce a mellow, woody effect.

Another approach could be to use bog and marginal plants as well as some shrubs to provide more colour and a generally overgrown appearance. This second idea would need slightly better light levels than the ferns, which do well under trees.

" The cave
shown here is set into
a natural bank "

ABOVE: A cave and
cascade in a wood-
land setting with
ferns and mosses

Building up sides

The back, sides and entrance to the
cave are built up on the edges of the
pool and the two plinths. Rock must be
mortared together but with joints
'raked out' so that no mortar is visible
once construction is complete.

The back and parts of the sides of
the cave could well be up against an
excavated bank of soil, and if there are
to be steps on one or both sides, as
shown here, these must be created at
the same time, using the same chunky
pieces of rock.

You should try and build a 'fair' face
of rockwork around the inside of the
cave and also on either side of the
entrance, and this may mean having to
use two rocks back-to-back in places

on an extra thick section of foundation.

To give it a more natural appearance, mortar boulders onto the floor of
the pool and incorporate some
planting pockets.

Water will not come up above the
level of the concrete shell, but rocks
will almost certainly be needed around
the front of the pool – in front of the
cave – to hold back soil, especially if
the whole feature has been set down
into the ground.

In the example here, some modest
terraces or steps have been created
down to the water's edge. Whether this
terracing is filled with soil or stones
will depend upon whether a planted
area or a stony beach is wanted.

Once the sides have been built up
to the required height, the lintel can
be lifted up and mortared into position to complete this particular stage

of the construction.

If the cave is not having water and
may therefore attract young children
inside, the lintel should be set on a
piece of steel bar for extra safety.

Roof

One of the easiest ways to make the
roof is to pack the cave temporarily
with sealed plastic bags of compost until
they are within about 15cm (6in) from
the top edge of the sides and lintel.

Over the bags is laid a sheet of polythene and then a whole covering of thin,
flattish rocks. These rocks will eventually
produce a stony roof to the cave.

Concrete is then poured over the
flat rocks into this 15cm-deep cavity
with steel reinforcing incorporated
through the centre.

Ideally, the underside of this roof
section should arch upwards slightly so
that the roof of the cave is not flat. The
concrete should be slightly runny so
that it can flow and be pushed into all
the corners as well as grip the flat rocks
underneath.

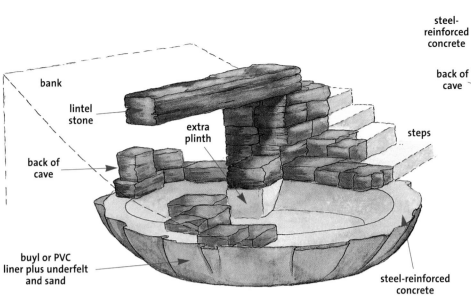

bank

lintel
stone

back of
cave

extra
plinth

steps

buyl or PVC
liner plus underfelt
and sand

steel-reinforced
concrete

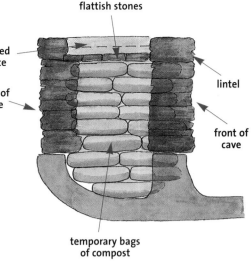

flattish stones

steel-
reinforced
concrete

back of
cave

lintel

front of
cave

temporary bags
of compost

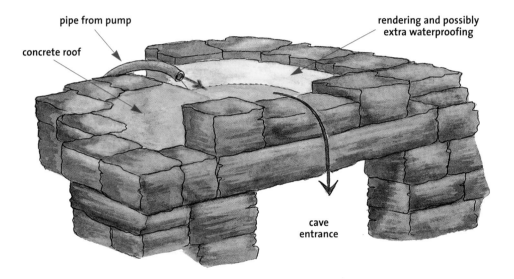

pipe from pump

concrete roof

rendering and possibly
extra waterproofing

cave
entrance

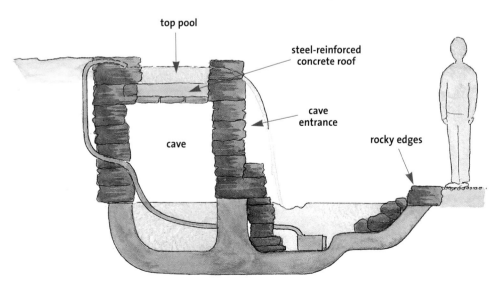

top pool

steel-reinforced
concrete roof

cave
entrance

cave

rocky edges

The more rugged the rocks are
around the edges the better, since this
will ensure that the completed concrete
roof can never drop down into the
pool below!

Concreting is finished off flush and
flat – and preferably level – with the top
edges of the surrounding rocks and
lintel. Once the concrete has set, the
compost bags can be carefully pulled out
of the way to leave a fully formed cave.

Upper pool

More rocks can now be mortared onto
the top, around the edges, to create a
shallow rock pool. A lower stone must
be incorporated over the central part of
the lintel so that water can flow out
here and down into the pool below.

On their own these rocks will not
hold water, so the whole of the upper
pool must be rendered with sharp sand
and cement.

In addition it could be treated with a
waterproofing product like G4, or
perhaps GRP (glass-reinforced plastic –
fibreglass). This is used by professional
pool experts to line all manner of water
features. If you want to use this technique, try *Yellow Pages* to get in touch
with a glass-fibre moulding company.
They may well have someone on their
staff who would come out to your
garden and line the finished rock pool
for you. It is not a cheap option, but it
is probably the best one.

A pipe from the submersible pump
in the main pool has to be incorporated
into the fabric of the upper pool as
discreetly as possible, and of course, a
suitable and equally discreet electricity
supply will be needed to run the pump
and perhaps some of the lighting too.

The top pool will look most effective if it is part of a larger area of
rocks running in from the ground
around. It will look less convincing as
an isolated little pool literally stuck on
top of the cave.

66 ***To give it a more natural appearance
mortar boulders onto the floor of the pool and
incorporate some planting pockets*** *99*

Life's a beach for birds

There is more than one way of constructing a beach for your pond

If child safety does not have to be a consideration, a traditional pond can offer great scope for the creation of different interesting features around it. Particularly effective is a beach, either sandy or stony to resemble a section of sea shore or muddy to set the scene for a completely different range of plants.

Boulders, pebbles, shells and so on can be introduced to give the effect of the foreshore, and this beach could be extended far beyond the actual confines of the pond into an area where deck chairs might be set up on the sand, where an upturned boat lies between large rocks and where surrounding plants reflect the type of vegetation likely to be found by the sea shore; maybe the garden shed could be made to look like a beach hut!

On a more limited scale the beach may be extended no further than the pool liner while still featuring pebbles, boulders and rock pools.

The only real limitation is that algae might grow in some of the shallow water at the height of summer – something which rarely happens in the constantly washed pools of salty water on the shore.

This algae can often be controlled by using an algicide from time to time. The shallow water, stones and marginal

PICTURES: HARRY SMITH COLLECTION

"The shallow water, stones and marginal planting will certainly attract more wildlife – including more newts, frogs, toads and birds like the grey wagtail – than a conventional pool-side"

LEFT: Pebble beach in the making over plastic liner

This Chelsea Flower Show garden uses sympathetic naturalistic planting to enhance the seaside vision

"Never use dark yellow building sand - it is too mucky and murky. A fine washed, perhaps silver, sand is better"

RIGHT: Merrist Wood College came up with this 'seaside' design for a Chelsea Flower Show

planting will certainly attract more wildlife – including more newts, frogs, toads and birds like the grey wagtail – than a conventional pool-side.

The water level is bound to fluctuate from time to time but, providing the feature is designed and built to accommodate this, a variable water level will add to the interest as various parts of the beach appear and disappear.

Unlike the sandy

beach which has, for the most part, an open, light feeling about it, the muddy beach is likely to fit more naturally into shrubby and wooded surroundings.

Instead of large stones and boulders this beach could have old tree stumps on mossy mounds. Clayey mud

could attract house martins searching for building materials.

Whichever type of beach is wanted, the pond will have to be designed and built – or

adapted – to accommodate what will in fact be a large dedicated area comprising mostly a flat shelf 25cm (9in) or so below the maximum water level of the pond.

It can only be added to an existing pond if a means can be found of joining the new section onto the old so that it is completely watertight.

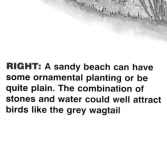

RIGHT: A sandy beach can have some ornamental planting or be quite plain. The combination of stones and water could well attract birds like the grey wagtail

BELOW: A muddy beach can be planted to blend in with the surrounding garden. House martins may visit the beach for nest-building materials

Designing a beach

It is quite possible that the beach will occupy at least as much space as the pond itself. If a liner is used, this means extending it several feet or metres in one particular direction.

Creating a beach all the way around a pond can be a mistake since, under some circumstances, it could end up looking like a partially dried up puddle.

Having the beach on one side of the pond only should make it possible to have relatively deep water directly opposite – a more realistic situation.

If a butyl or PVC liner is being used, it must have an underfelt; also, because stones, sand, mud or even tree stumps will be placed on top, a layer of PVC should be placed directly over the liner.

Excavation for the beach area should begin alongside the garden/lawn with a vertical cut going down about 15-25cm (6-9in). It can slope very slightly down towards the main area of the pool before finally going down at about 45° into the deep

part – to a depth of at least 45cm (18in).

The liner and its underfelt are laid across the area – first making sure that there are no sharp protruding objects – and across the remainder of the pool excavation.

When eventually the pool is filled right up, there must be sufficient spare liner to protrude vertically up against the adjacent garden/lawn by at least 1cm (½in) all the way around. It is a good idea to first fill the main body of the pool up as far as the edge of the shelf so that the liner can settle and stretch.

Constructing muddy beach

For a muddy beach, you will need to build a fairly solid retaining wall of dead turf about 15cm (6in) high and about 15cm (6in) back from the 45° drop.

The bottom turf can be completely unravelled and draped over the edge down into the deeper section. This will hide the butyl liner in the unlikely event that the water

level ever drops that low.

A heavy clay loam is then used to fill the area between the turf wall and the vertical portion of liner next to the garden/lawn. Once the soil has been compacted and levelled off it should be at the same level as the adjacent garden soil/lawn and slope slightly down to the top of the turf wall.

Once this general level has been established, slightly higher and lower areas can be created and any stumps or whatever added to look as natural as possible.

You can sometimes find 'star'-shaped stumps where the roots have been partially rotted away, and one of these can have quite an architectural appearance as

well as look interesting planted with ferns etc.

To give interest to the beach whatever the water level in the pond, the whole area must be 'landscaped' – even if part of it will be under water sometimes.

Constructing sandy beach

Construction of the sandy beach is similar to that for the muddy beach – with some important differences.

The shaping of the shelf is the same but excavation may continue on the outside (garden/lawn side) of the liner so that sand 15cm (6in) deep can replace the soil and extend the beach further up into the garden as a feature.

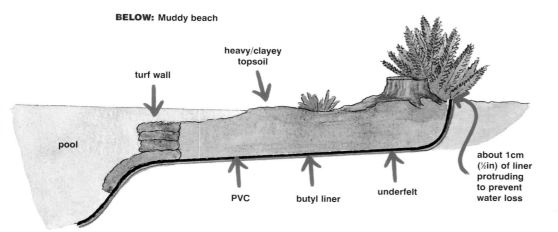

turf wall

heavy/clayey topsoil

pool

PVC

butyl liner

underfelt

about 1cm (½in) of liner protruding to prevent water loss

"The muddy beach provides far more flexibility since it is likely to fit in to a whole range of existing garden layouts"

This area will of course never be influenced by the pond water since it is beyond the lined area. Once again, the top surface of the liner must be protected by some PVC sheeting and beneath by its underfelt.

Instead of a turf wall, one made from stone or small boulders is more appropriate. This must be set on a generous bed of mortar and be mortared together. Its position and height should be the same as for the turf wall, but don't worry if some of the stones end up a little higher.

Ideally, about 7.5cm (3in) of stone-free sandy subsoil should first go onto the shelf; top off with well-compacted sand. Alternatively, if the subsoil is not available, the whole depth can be in sand.

Never use dark yellow building sand – it is too mucky and murky. A fine washed, perhaps silver, sand is better,

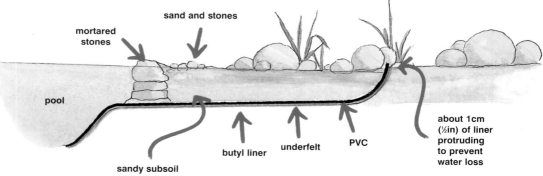

BELOW: Sandy beach

mortared stones

sand and stones

pool

sandy subsoil

butyl liner

underfelt

PVC

about 1cm (½in) of liner protruding to prevent water loss

although there is the possibility that this type of sand may be moved around by bathing birds.

Use only smooth stones, pebbles and rounded boulders, similar to those found on a beach, arranging them as if the sea has washed away from them, leaving the lower half of larger stones still buried. Boulders usually look better in groups or clusters rather than dotted about singly, and some areas of sand can be left lower so that water forms pools whenever the pond is full.

Also consider placing such objects as lobster pots, large shells, a fishing net and some suitably water-worn pieces of driftwood.

Planting

Neither kind of beach will look right unless the planting for some distance away is appropriate. Imagine the state a sandy beach would get into were it to be created near, for example, an apple tree – leaves and rotten fruit everywhere.

For a sandy beach, the most appropriate planting is likely to be small to medium-sized ornamental grasses, with plants like phormium, cordyline and yucca in the background.

Although there shouldn't be any messy deciduous trees close by, a dwarf pine, Spanish gorse and some other small evergreen shrubs can look effective.

Tall grasses too – including the relatively small pampas *Cortaderia selloana* 'Pumila' – can be useful background plants.

Planting does not necessarily have to be highly ornamental. A trip to an unspoiled stretch of coastline will reveal a native range and arrangement of plants which could be re-created in the garden along with some small imitation dunes.

The muddy beach provides far more flexibility since it is likely to fit in to a whole range of existing garden layouts. Ferns, mosses, trailing plants and small marginal plants are ideal for the beach itself.

Ajuga reptans cultivars, *Lysimachia nummularia* 'Aurea' and small-leafed ivies are all more appropriate for the muddy beach.

The surrounding area could have a selection of bog plants, small shrubs and perhaps some small conifers gradually blending in with the rest of the garden.

This general cover of plants is important not just for its appearance, as it will provide useful cover for creatures travelling to and from the beach.

MAINTENANCE

■ Apart from the problem of algae, weeds will grow readily on all 'beaches', especially grass which can come from a mower throwing out seeds from a nearby lawn; avoid using a hover-type mower near the beach.

■ Debris must be removed regularly, especially from a sandy beach – it can help to net the area just before leaf fall so that it stays relatively clean during the autumn.

■ Dogs and cats may be a nuisance, so may need to be kept away with some form of deterrent.

■ Do remember that a beach will attract the curiosity of young children and could therefore lure them into deeper water.

Water feature with an oriental flavour

Oriental thinking

'**O**riental' is probably one of the most popular themes for garden features today – especially for small gardens, although the way in which 'oriental' is interpreted seems to vary widely.

In their countries of origin these gardens provide their owners with peace of mind, inspiration, and somewhere to meditate. All the component parts of the garden mean something – the position of carefully selected boulders, lanterns, stone figures, raked gravel, plants, and of course water, real or imaginary.

In the western world a true appreciation of the deeper meaning behind these things is difficult, but we do enjoy the serenity and peace that the gardens can give.

Commission

I was asked by a couple who had spent many years in oriental regions of the world, to create a water feature with an oriental flavour to remind them of their times overseas. It was to be somewhere where they could sit peacefully in the evening sun, watch and listen to the sound of moving water, and enjoy surroundings which at least had a hint of the orient.

The result, some years later, is complete with its beautiful, though quite expensive, carved bridge.

The peace and tranquillity of an oriental garden can be recreated even in a small space

Planning

To create a feature like this, which must look as far as possible as if it has always been there, requires some very careful planning – this one has been built within a butyl liner.

The overall design had to incorporate the bridge and therefore a path, a wider area of paving for a bench, virtually seamless planting from the garden borders down into the water, boulders, pebbles, a pebbly stream, and seclusion.

Luckily, the corner of the garden where it was to go was already quite secluded, so it did not take much extra planting to complete that part of it. Some of the planting was to be marginal and boggy, so areas of soil which were actually in water had to be introduced.

Other borders were to have a variety of planting, but especially ornamental grasses, irises and fragrant plants.

"To create a feature like this, which must look as far as is possible is if it has always been there, requires some very careful planning"

ABOVE: The carved bridge was an expensive, but beautiful, addition

There was some debate as to whether a pond filter was needed and in the end it was decided to have quite a large one together with a facility for pool lighting, and a heater to prevent freezing in case fish were introduced.

Fortunately the ground was almost perfectly level which always helps to make a water feature look as if it should be there. It was also decided to use butyl rather than concrete, but that the liner should be completely invisible, even at low tide! Apart from the main pond, there had to be a stream over which the bridge could go and from where water could flow noisily over stones and pebbles.

The pool

To create seamless planting right down into the water requires an underwater shelf. Its width must bear some relationship to the overall size of the pond. In this case the pond was about 5.5m (18ft) across so it seemed reasonable to have shelves that were about 50cm (20in) wide.

The shelf was to accommodate soil and sometimes stones so it needed to start off at least 10cm (4in) deep up against the surrounding garden, and slope gently down so that most of the

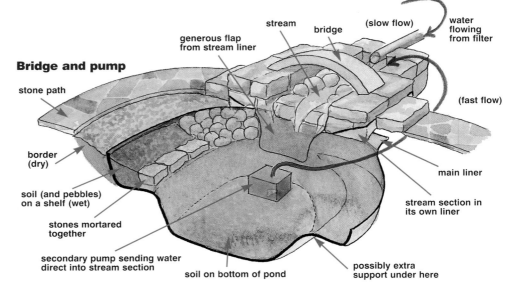

Bridge and pump

- stone path
- border (dry)
- soil (and pebbles) on a shelf (wet)
- stones mortared together
- secondary pump sending water direct into stream section
- generous flap from stream liner
- stream
- bridge
- (slow flow)
- water flowing from filter
- (fast flow)
- main liner
- stream section in its own liner
- possibly extra support under here
- soil on bottom of pond

soil would in fact be under water – unless the water level dropped significantly.

All this shaping was cut from firm virgin soil but some extra support was needed under the liner in the form of timber edging to prevent the edge of the shelf from eventually collapsing. One liner was used for the pond and another, overlapping generously with the first, was used for the stream section. A generous layer of under-felt must always be used under a liner, especially where it goes over any timber edging or stony ground.

Building

This pond was made about 80cm (2ft 8in) deep in the centre. About 75mm (3in) of heavy clay

soil had to be placed in the bottom of the pond – this could be dead, upturned turves – to ensure that the liner would remain weighted down and did not become stretched or 'stressed' once the shelves had been filled.

A strip of black PVC about

15cm (6in) wide was then placed over the butyl quite close to the edge of the shelf – about 38mm (1½in) – and back from it so that a row of stones could be mortared all round to prevent the soil and stones from washing down into the bottom of the

MAINTENANCE

Neither scheme could be regarded as very low maintenance, but a few points taken into account right at the beginning can help to cut down on the eventual maintenance...
1. Sighting the feature well away from large trees will help to minimise the problem of autumn leaves.
2. Any soil brought into the pond should be clayey rather than silty so that the filter does not clog up with silt. This is a problem that can occur if lots of dead turves are used.
3. Bamboos and other rampant plants can be grown within a piece of liner or in a hidden container to limit their spread.
4. The use of a weed mat under stones and gravel can be very effective here especially as it will seldom be walked on.

Plan view of the main feature (not to scale)

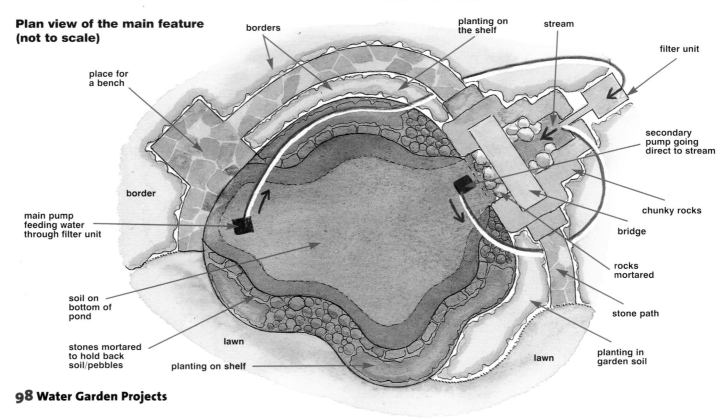

- borders
- planting on the shelf
- stream
- filter unit
- place for a bench
- secondary pump going direct to stream
- border
- chunky rocks
- main pump feeding water through filter unit
- bridge
- rocks mortared
- soil on bottom of pond
- stone path
- stones mortared to hold back soil/pebbles
- lawn
- planting on shelf
- lawn
- planting in garden soil

pond. The PVC prevents the mortar from actually sticking to the liner and 'stressing' it.

Some sections of the shelf were filled right up with soil, level with the adjacent garden, and others were only half-filled so that there was room for a beach of stones and pebbles.

As the liner emerged vertically from the back of the shelf, excess butyl was trimmed off, leaving about 1cm (½in) upstanding to prevent wet soil on the shelf from coming into contact with the relatively dry garden soil. If this were to happen, water would be constantly lost from the pond.

The stream section was lined with stones and boulders, with those nearest the main pond being mortared for stability. Large flat boulders were arranged on either side of the stream to accommodate the bridge and form steps.

Pumps

As soon as construction was complete a powerful submersible pump, with a flow valve, was lowered into the pond as far from the stream as possible so that a circulation could be established right across the pond.

At first the pipe was fed straight into the rocks at the back of the stream and this produced a really vigorous flow crashing its way over all the stones. However, once this pipe had been connected to the filter, the water flowing out from there into the stream had little or no force behind it and was visually very disappointing.

To get a forceful flow back, a second smaller pump was installed just below the 'waterfall' and fed directly into the top of the stream to join water coming from the filter. Most filters are ugly and need hiding, but fortunately existing shrubs already provided some screening so it did not take much to complete the job.

Planting

If this were to have been a truly traditional oriental feature then the planting would have been minimal. Most of the shelves would have carried stones down into the water and individual bonsai trees might well have been used as the only planting, except perhaps for a backdrop of bamboos or grasses.

As it happened, planting was not to be minimal here, but quite full. The shelves were planted with irises, primulas, calceolaria, *Lobelia cardinalis*, dwarf ornamental grasses and a truly dwarf bamboo. The adjacent borders continued this theme but had to reflect much drier soil conditions.

A small weeping tree – *Caragana arborescens pendula* 'Walker' – created height on one side and a Japanese maple on the other. Because this feature was only one corner in an otherwise conventional garden, 'ordinary' garden plants were never far away, but the addition of some ornamental bamboos helped to blur the transition.

SMALLER GARDEN

The second 'oriental' water feature shown here takes much less space and is simpler. There is no bridge or stream, and the planting is far more minimal. Large smooth boulders create some height along with a weeping tree and some bamboo.

The bamboo screen is important because it helps to set the scene, along with the lantern. Although there are a few grasses and messy plants, most of the plants are individual specimens, like the Japanese maple in the foreground. Some bonsai trees would look especially effective in these surroundings.

This pond, like the previous one, has pebbles down to the water's edge and beyond, but very little marginal planting. This would be achieved in exactly the same way as in the larger garden.

There is no flow of water and this could lead to the formation of algae and stagnation so it would be important to have a good range of aquatic plants – some oxygenating plants and perhaps some water lilies to reduce the amount of sunlight entering the water.

A modest flow could be introduced using water flowing out from a bamboo chute or by using a 'deer scarer' where water fills up a section of bamboo stem which then tips and knocks on a stone. Both will of course need an electrical supply and a small submersible pump.

bamboo screen
large boulders
bonsai
bamboo
lantern
Caragana arborescens pendula 'Walker'
Japanese maple
gravel/pebbles
stepping stones

A simpler approach, but just as effective

"If this were to have been a truly traditional oriental feature then the planting would have been minimal"

ABOVE: Bamboo chute can be used for a modest flow of water

Building bridges

As these stylish examples show, a bridge should be more than merely a structure used to cross a pond or stream

Not only is a bridge attractive to look at, especially if water is visibly flowing beneath it, but it also opens up the possibility of a new walkway within the garden.

Some water features may not of course be suitable for a bridge – they may be too wide or too tiny – but most could take a bridge if it was in an appropriate size or style.

Even if the bridge is not strong or large enough to walk over, it might still be worth having as a purely visual feature.

If it is to be a walkway then it must be strong – robust enough to support a heavy adult, and possibly wide enough for a mower. The bridge must be planned into the existing garden layout so that a path can follow a sensible route to and from it.

Although bridges come in all styles, they fall into two main categories – arched or flat, although many 'flat' bridges do often have a slight curve.

Flat bridges

These are the easiest to construct. At their simplest they could be a large slab of stone or a couple of railway sleepers side by side. In both these cases, but particularly in the case of the stone slab, the span will have to be fairly limited.

Being flat, these bridges will be only just above the water's surface unless the water is at a lower level – say running along a ditch.

Safety can pose another problem since it may not be easy to attach a handrail, especially to a bridge made from a slab of stone.

However, despite these limitations and their simplicity, such bridges can still be attractive and useful features, specially if they are landscaped into their surroundings properly.

This can be achieved by making sure that they fit into the bank on either side, link with some kind of path and have some planting around either end.

More elaborate flat bridges will often be in the form of a narrow deck, with timber planks fixed down onto a sub frame, and with handrails of some description.

These can, therefore, span much greater distances than slabs of stone and, despite being flat, can have a slight curve styled into them. They can be built 'off site' in a workshop before being slotted into position.

There are many styles to mimic – classic, oriental, modern and so on – with the styling of the handrails playing an important part in the overall effect.

Most timber structures these days are made from pressure-treated softwood. Several of the pressure-treatment chemicals are, however, toxic to wildlife and when using this treated timber to make a bridge it is possible that some of the chemical could wash out into the water below.

There are two or three ways around this. Use hardwood which may need no treatment,

ABOVE: This bridge is one of the simplest to construct, using a couple of old railway sleepers

LEFT: A typical rustic bridge in a garden setting

ABOVE: Bricks and timber make a naturalistic bridge in this 1999 Hampton Court Palace Flower Show garden

RIGHT: Timber bridge in the Japanese style at Hampton Court '99

or coat the finished, pressure-treated bridge – once it has completely dried – with Sadolin Classic or something similar, which may well seal in the pressure treatment. Alternatively, untreated softwood could be used and thoroughly treated with a non-toxic material.

Curved bridges

Generally these are more intricate to build than a flat bridge; although curved bridges could also be in timber they are more commonly built in brick or various types of stone.

They are ideally suited to span a ditch or stream where the bulk of the bridge goes down into the ditch, creating something of a tunnel or culvert.

The top of the bridge may then be almost at ground level and therefore curved. The higher the bridge is above water, and therefore further out of the ground, the more hump-backed it will become. Curved timber bridges can of course be bought ready made.

Other curved bridges made from stone or brick have to be built up in situ. One of the first decisions to make must be whether to build the bridge within the pond structure/liner or span it from outside.

Reasons of safety may dictate a handrail, and this may need careful designing to ensure that it does not look at odds with the bridge. A curved bridge will often be stronger than a flat one.

ABOVE: Paving stones used in the construction of this bridge are continued in an attractive winding path

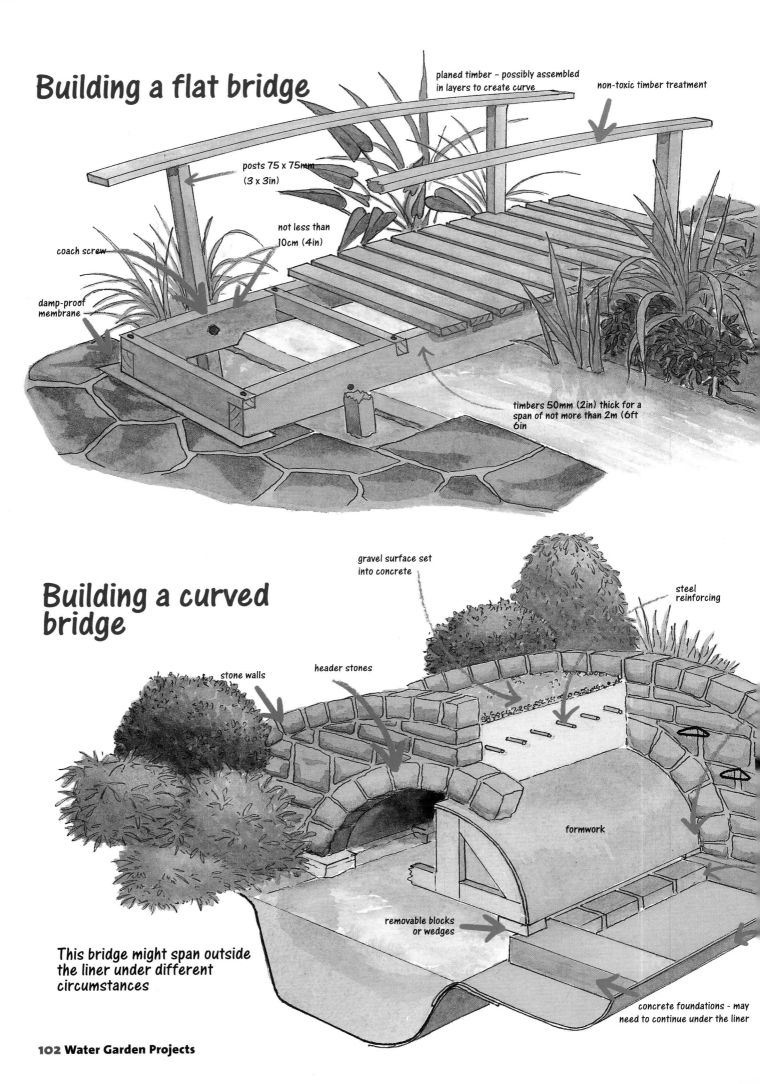

Building a flat bridge

planed timber – possibly assembled in layers to create curve

non-toxic timber treatment

posts 75 x 75mm (3 x 3in)

not less than 10cm (4in)

coach screw

damp-proof membrane

timbers 50mm (2in) thick for a span of not more than 2m (6ft 6in

Building a curved bridge

gravel surface set into concrete

steel reinforcing

stone walls

header stones

formwork

This bridge might span outside the liner under different circumstances

removable blocks or wedges

concrete foundations - may need to continue under the liner

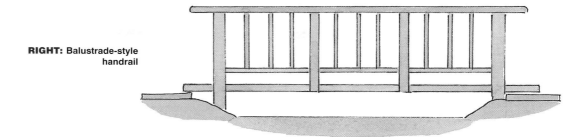

RIGHT: Balustrade-style handrail

'poured' concrete - no thinner than 150mm (6in)

steel ties

brick or stone infill - not always necessary

(the liner must be thoroughly protected from all pressures and puncturing)

BUILDING A FLAT BRIDGE

The flat bridge illustrated here is composed of two main load-bearing beams joined by some cross members and decking. The bridge must be supported in two ways: firstly by resting either end on a modest but firm foundation; secondly – and more importantly – by bolting the bridge to four stout uprights planted firmly into the ground to rise up above the bridge and support the handrail.

The effective span bearing the full load will then be between these uprights and not between the extreme ends of the bridge.

Timber thicknesses

The two load-bearing beams must be at least 5cm (2in) thick and never less than 10cm (4in) deep between the two main load-bearing points between the uprights, over a span of up to 2m (6ft 6in).

This means that, taking into account any cutting or styling which could take place in this zone, the plank of timber will probably have to start out 15cm (6in) deep.

The top edge of the beam can be cut to a slight curve and notched to take three or four shorter cross beams.

More styling might take place along the bottom edge, but this must never reduce the effective depth below 10cm (4in). It helps to draw this main beam to scale on paper so that all the cuts and styling can be carefully planned and minimum depths guaranteed.

The shorter cross members – representing the width of the bridge – should not be less than 38mm (1^1/$_2$in) thick, and about

5cm (2in) deep. They will be notched at either end so that they can lap and be fixed into the notches cut along the top of each main beam.

Fixing is best done with some substantial rust-resistant screws, but for extra rigidity brackets could be added to the underside.

The decking planks should run transversely across the bridge and be about 25mm (1in) thick and 50 to 75mm (2 to 3in) wide, with a gap of 10 to 12mm (^{3}/$_8$ to ^{1}/$_2$in) between each, and an overhang at either end of up to 38mm (1^1/$_2$in).

They can be fixed down with rust-resistant nails or screws, and will give the bridge its rigidity.

These decking planks can be in hardwood or softwood.

The four uprights or handrail supports should be about 75mm (3in) square, in planed or sawn timber. They must be fixed firmly into the ground so that the bridge fits snugly between them.

They can rise above the bridge to a comfortable handrail height and perhaps have their tops slightly angled to take the curved handrail.

The handrail should be the same width as the uprights – or slightly more – and could be cut to a curve from a solid piece of planed timber; alternatively, two or three bendy strips of planed timber can be glued, screwed and strapped together to form a curve which matches that of the bridge.

Once set and sanded, the two handrails can be screwed/fixed down onto the top of the posts.

Fixing into position

To discourage decay, where either end of the bridge touches a small foundation it should rest on a damp-proof membrane.

The most effective way of fixing the bridge between the uprights is to go in under the decking planks with coach screws.

These will pass through a hole in the main beam and screw right into the post. They should end up at least halfway into the post.

They are, in effect, heavy-duty screws which have to be 'wound' in and tightened with a spanner.

BUILDING A CURVED BRIDGE

The heart of any curved brick or stone bridge is the form-work which is used to create the curve.

There are various ways of making this but, essentially, it is a curved former made from wood and board the width of the bridge, over which the materials are laid.

After construction has been completed, this formwork has to be slipped out, so it must be set up on small blocks or wedges which can be removed, allowing the form-work to drop and slide out.

The curved portion of the formwork will have to be covered with 'building' paper or something similar to prevent the construction materials from sticking to it.

Four concrete strip foundations are needed – two for each end of the bridge. The

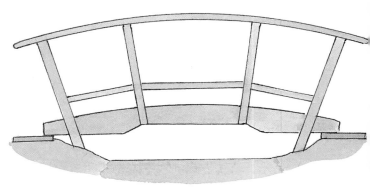

ABOVE: Handrails styled to match a curved bridge

ABOVE: Rope and timber at this Down Under-style garden at the 1999 Hampton Court show

BELOW: Metal handrails bolted into stonework

position of these will depend upon the overall position of the bridge in relation to the water.

The formwork is designed to sit on the inner edge of these foundations – on the wedges or blocks.

Header stones and walling are built up simultaneously at either end, incorporating some steel ties to stick out into the space created between the two walls.

These walls are built up just a little higher than the planned surface of the bridge so that it ends up with a kerb on either side.

Once the walls have set, concrete can be carefully poured and built up between them, incorporating some steel rein-

forcing and the ties on its way.

The steel, in the form of a grid or rods, must be at least two aggregate stones in from the nearest surface.

The concrete can either become the finished surface, perhaps with a gravel dressing,

or it could be stopped below the finished level and topped with some form of paving.

This type of bridge does not always have a handrail but, should one be needed, steel often works better than timber.

Once the concrete has set,

the formwork can be removed to leave a perfectly formed bridge. Happy crossing!

> **Timber thicknesses given are only a guide and may need to be increased to cope with additional stresses. Timber varies in quality**

ABOVE: Curved walking surface provides interest to this plank bridge

ABOVE: You could just step across but the bridge provides an extra focal point

The Woodland Waters garden
at Hampton Court Flower Show, 1999

A garden with a Moroccan or Moorish influence using many hardy or half-hardy plants with an 'exotic' appearance – the trees are in neighbouring gardens and the plot is at least partially walled. Plot size is about 8.5m (28ft) wide and 11.5m (38ft) long

Road to

The Moorish style of North Africa is the inspiration for this stylish garden which is quite at home in a cooler climate

Some of the 'exotic' gardens fashionable today are exotic in a jungly sort of way, with lots of ferns, small palms and other lush green plants in a damp, mossy setting. Others are exotic and 'hot', with lots of bright colours, succulents, pebbles, stones and arid surroundings. But now for something just a little different – a garden with a Moroccan or Moorish theme.

Because it is hot in Morocco many of the gardens are designed to provide a cool and restful haven out of the baking sun. This is not to say that there are no bright colours – there are – but more important is the shade afforded by palms, small trees, shrubs and vigorous climbers scrambling over an overhead structure of some sort.

"While my interpretation is not perhaps entirely authentic, it could easily be recreated in a smallish British garden using materials and plants more suited to our own climate"

ABOVE: The Moorish theme can be extended to borders. A blue mosaic-lined pool lies in front of the triangular wall

Morocco

While my interpretation is not perhaps entirely authentic, it could easily be recreated in a smallish British garden using materials and plants more suited to our own climate.

Mine is a garden of contrasts, providing some shade – partly from overhanging neighbouring trees – and other parts which will be in full sun for much of the day.

Raised beds
Although the plot is basically flat, the garden has been created on different levels. There are two raised beds, each about 40cm (16in) high. One runs across the far end of the garden and is curved, and the other is on the left, closer to the house.

The retaining walls are made from concrete blocks rendered and decorated white. In our climate these will probably need redecorating annually.

Where there is already a boundary garden wall these beds can be built up against it but fences would, of course, have to be protected by a retaining wall running around the back of each raised bed.

Patio, loggia
The third raised area is a patio. Its floor is only about 15cm (6in) above the main garden level and is tiled with blue/grey ceramic tiles – which could become slippery when wet.

Set into this floor is a series of thick, rounded supports for the loggia, which has been designed to have a slightly Turkish look about it.

The shaped panels around the top are made from thick 'exterior' ply which will last many years outdoors. A thin edging strip has been fixed along the top and bottom edges and the main area clad with trellis.

All the timber must be thoroughly treated with a colourless

> **"The fountain is a small geyser-jet rather than a 'spray' type since a jet is likely to be more stable and therefore less wasteful on windy days"**

about 8.5m (28ft) wide

about 11.5m (38ft) long

raised shrub border including *Morus nigra* (mulberry), syringa (lilac), *Chamaerops humilis*, *Fatsia japonica*

pebbled surface exposed aggregate concrete

pool and fountain

mostly herbaceous planting

edging of small setts or blocks

loggia over raised tiled patio with vines

rill

step

raised border with pots, lavender etc

removable slate over reservoir

step

pebble mosaic path

grey paved patio

'total' timber preservative before being stained – in this case light blue, dark blue and grey.

Heavy cross-beams support vigorous climbers and the whole structure runs alongside a high, white, rendered wall and will soon become a cool and shady place to sit.

Water feature

The whole of the water feature is best made from concrete. This will need reinforcing with steel, especially since the long 'rill' will be rather vulnerable to cracking. The concrete will then need rendering. It could also be lined with GRP (see page 90) if you are not using ceramic tiles.

Despite all this, concrete is probably still a better option than a butyl liner. The pool and rill are edged with a double row of grey setts or small blocks. These must not overhang the edge by more than about 1cm (½in), otherwise those along the very edge could become unstable.

The rill needs a concealed reservoir at the 'bottom' end in order to accommodate the pump. Water is then pumped along to the pool and fountain in order to create a flow.

The pipe could run along the bottom of the rill but it will need disguising with stones or peb-

bles. A narrow slot could quite easily be cast into the concrete to take the pipe. The fountain is a small geyser-jet rather than a 'spray' type since a jet is likely to be more stable and therefore less wasteful on windy days.

The whole system must be dead level and a removable cover – perhaps a piece of slate – should be placed over the reservoir so that the pump can be serviced from time to time. An electricity supply is also needed, discreetly installed nearby.

A feature like this would look especially attractive lined with blue mosaic tiles and it would be more usual to have it completely devoid of any plants or pond life, making the use of some form of wildlife-safe sterilant or algaecide necessary to ensure that the water remains crystal clear.

Paved area

Around the water feature is an area of concrete paving which has been cast between edging setts and given a surface rich in flinty-coloured stones.

To achieve this, all the edging setts must first be protected with thin polythene. The excavated area, perhaps deep enough to allow for about 10cm (4in) of concrete over a hard-core base, is then filled to within about 2.5cm (1in) of the top with a standard concrete mix (one part cement plus six parts all-in ballast).

Then, straight away, a special mix using white cement and a high proportion of grey stone is laid on top to complete the final 2.5cm.

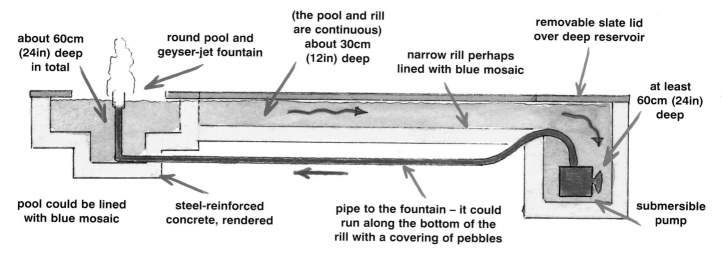

about 60cm (24in) deep in total

round pool and geyser-jet fountain

(the pool and rill are continuous) about 30cm (12in) deep

narrow rill perhaps lined with blue mosaic

removable slate lid over deep reservoir

at least 60cm (24in) deep

pool could be lined with blue mosaic

steel-reinforced concrete, rendered

pipe to the fountain – it could run along the bottom of the rill with a covering of pebbles

submersible pump

"Pots, urns and rounded stones are used throughout the garden to create extra points of interest"

ABOVE: Barley-sugar pillars and a colourful pot accent a Moorish feel

HARRY SMITH COLLECTION

After a few hours the surface can be very gently washed and brushed to expose the stones. A few days later an acid wash can be used to clean and brighten up the surface of the stones. Finally the polythene can be cut away from the edging setts. If the inside of the feature is to be tiled, it would be wise to delay that until the concreting is complete.

Pebble mosaic

This area of the garden is connected to the rest by a mosaic path. The diamond pattern is simply achieved by pressing dark or light grey pebbles into a mortar bed, taking care to avoid too much mortar oozing up between the stones.

Pots, urns and rounded stones are used throughout the garden to create extra points of interest.

With just a little stretch of the imagination you could be in that great Moorish-influenced piece of Spanish architecture, the Alhambra.

Planting

You will see a huge range of plants in Morocco, and these will vary considerably depending on where you are.

In the more arid areas, lavender covers the hillsides. In other parts, where there is more moisture available, there are magnificent drifts of gladioli, irises, lupins, poppies, orange marigolds and other species producing a whole tapestry of colours.

In addition there are olives, walnuts, mulberries, almonds, citrus and cypress trees as well as lilac, mock orange blossom and a wealth of magnificent climbers.

Many of these plants will flourish in our own gardens, so it is not that difficult to piece together a reasonably authentic planting scheme. Despite all these bright colours, our garden here has been limited to cool greens, blues and greys.

In the raised bed across the far end of the garden is a *Chamaerops humilis* (dwarf palm) a syringa (lilac), a *Morus nigra* (mulberry), a *Fatsia japonica* and various other mainly green ground-covering plants.

To the left in full sun is a ground-level border of mainly herbaceous flowers including blue lupins and blue flag irises.

Closer to the house in another raised bed are some lavenders, *Convolvulus cneorum*, purple sage with various pots and pebbles.

To the right, a vigorous black grape is growing on the wall and up onto the loggia roof. The lemon tree in a pot would of course need winter protection. Also on the right is a *Trachycarpus fortunei*, a fig and more irises. Many seasonal or annual flowers could be added, but only if these fitted into the chosen colour scheme.

Apart from the citrus and perhaps the convolvulus, all these plants should be relatively hardy and easy to look after.

The vine will need training and pruning and, eventually, the trachycarpus could develop into quite a tall tree. The whole garden, and in particular the planting, could look stunning at night with the right sort of lighting.

All decked out

Garden decking need not be boring – here's how to turn it into a real feature

You would not believe how many boring decks I have seen in the past few years. Usually just a plain square or rectangle built tight up against the wall of the house with no space for plants and seldom any restraint around the edges to prevent chairs from toppling off. What has sometimes made matters even worse is the colour – that bright rusty 'cedar' red which bears no relationship to anything else in a garden and which is such a poor foil for most flower colours. Here are some ideas to help make an area of decking look more attractive and feel more comfortable to sit on.

Design

Even though a deck might need to be adjacent to some patio doors, it is not usually necessary to have the whole deck alongside the wall – only that portion which lines up with the door. The rest could be at least 45cm (18in) away from the house so that climbers and other plants can be grown to 'soften' the walls.

The main bulk of the deck must of course be large enough to accommodate garden furniture since it will not be possible, with the deck raised, to spread onto the surrounding lawn or paving. This does not necessarily mean that the whole deck has to be square. In this project a small, separate piece of decking is being used as a step to push the main deck away from the walls, and some simple shaping has been introduced to get away from a plain square without destroying the deck's usefulness. Some balustrading

has been introduced in places as an attractive way to prevent chairs, and people, from falling off – and around one corner balustrade uprights are extended to support a narrow double beam pergola for more climbers.

There are three stepping off points and a water feature which has two areas of interest linked by a 'stream' flowing beneath the deck. More planting spaces and a wooden trough help to ensure that the deck is not separate from the garden, but is very much part of it.

Building

There are many different ways of building a deck. Some methods involve highly 'professional' and sophisticated joints but the ideas here are comparatively simple, easy to achieve, yet robust and durable. Three main types of timber are used – sawn, pressure treated softwood for the ground supports and main framework of joists, the decking planks – often hardwood – and planed or 'prepared' smooth timber, needing some hand treatment with preservative, for balustrades.

Ground supports

In this particular project the deck is supported on a series of short pressure-treated posts, most of which will end up on the inside of the main frame. They are 10cm (4in) square and long enough to set into concrete, or into metal post sockets, as well as to hold the timber frame just clear of the ground. It is always good practice to paint extra preservative onto all the cut ends.

The top portion of each support can have a 'shelf' cut into it, perhaps 1cm (½in) wide, to help support each joist which will be screwed to it. If a shelf is not cut, the eventual

"Even though a deck might need to be adjacent to some patio doors, it is not usually necessary to have the whole deck alongside the wall"

joint will rely entirely on the screws and friction for its strength, which is not as good.

Frame

In this case the frame is made from pressure-treated timbers 5 by 15cm (2 by 6in) – although with extra support underneath

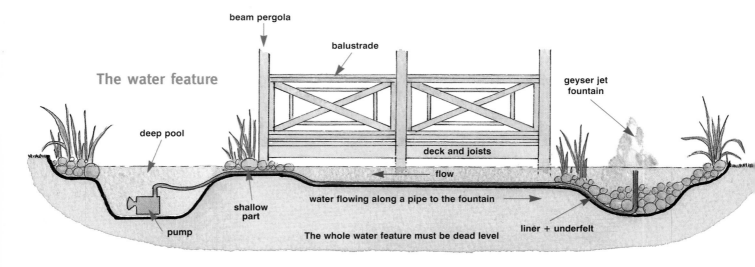

The water feature

beam pergola

balustrade

geyser jet fountain

deep pool

deck and joists

flow

shallow part

water flowing along a pipe to the fountain

pump

The whole water feature must be dead level

liner + underfelt

"It is fun having a deck going over water but this is not always easy to achieve because the decks supports can get in the way"

you might get away with 'joists' 5 by 10cm (2 by 4in). The outer framework of joists is screwed firmly to the ground supports, which must all be dead level and lined up exactly, followed by the intermediate joists fixed at intervals of about 40cm (16in) using 'joist hangers'. These are made from galvanised steel and can be purchased from most builders merchants. Some of these 'hangers' have long straps which will need shortening if they are not to show.

For extra rigidity a series of noggins can be nailed securely between the joists although decking planks will, in effect, help to do the same job once they are fixed in position.

Extra supports will be needed centrally under the deck, either in the form of extra timber ground supports or as brick/block plinths with a damp-proof membrane immediately beneath the joists. Without this extra support, the deck could sag.

Decking planks

The decking planks must be fixed down with a small and even gap between each – about 1cm. Although some can be nailed, it is worth remembering that valuables can fall between these planks and the only hope of retrieving them will be to have some of the planks screwed down with brass screws. Always use non-rusting hardware in a decking project.

Balustrade

The balustrade can be home-made or bought ready made. The supports here are 10 by 10cm (4 by 4in) 'prepared' or planed timber so they will actually end up slightly under the 10cm. They are fixed into metal post sockets, painted to match the balustrade, rather than more concrete.

The balustrade posts must line up down both sides, so to achieve this the corner support has been fixed to the main frame using a robust steel bracket. This, together with the post socket and adjoining balustrades will provide firm support. Some of the supports go to a height of about 2.25m (7ft 6in) and provide a fixing for the beam pergola.

Water feature

It is fun having a deck going over water but this is not always easy to achieve because the deck's supports can get in the way. Here, two areas of water are linked by a narrow 'stream' passing beneath the deck and between the supports. At one end is a geyser-type fountain among boulders and at the other, a pool with a pump. Water flows from the fountain towards the pool and where it emerges from under the deck, is quite shallow so that it can be seen bubbling over pebbles before arriving in the pond. The pond must be reasonably deep

ABOVE AND BELOW: There are a number of ways that decking can become more interesting and innovative

"Fragrance can come from climbers like summer jasmine and honeysuckle as well as from lilies, stocks and aromatic herbs grown in pots"

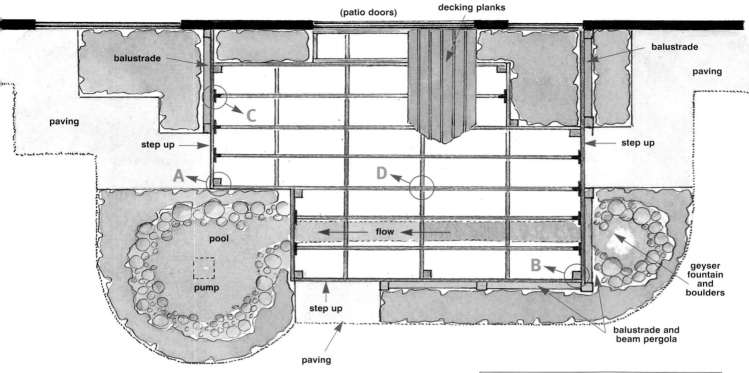

(patio doors)

decking planks

balustrade

balustrade

paving

paving

C

step up

step up

A

D

pool

flow

B

pump

geyser
fountain
and
boulders

step up

balustrade and
beam pergola

paving

A: Ground support

a small
"shelf"
about
1cm wide

main joists
screwed on

B: The corner balustrade post with a sturdy bracket fixing

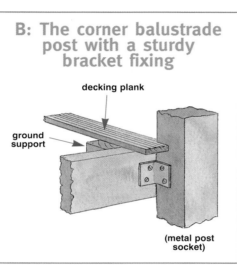

decking plank

ground
support

(metal post
socket)

C: Intermediate joists fixed with joist hangers

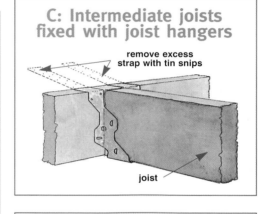

remove excess
strap with tin snips

joist

D: Noggins can be nailed opposite or staggered

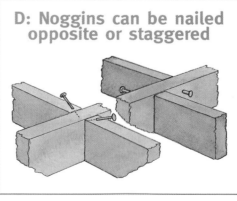

"There are three stepping off points and a water feature which has two areas of interest linked by a 'stream' flowing beneath the deck"

for the pump. A butyl liner is probably the most practical method of construction, with a thick underfelt. Care is needed to ensure the liner remains well hidden at the edges.

Colour scheme

There are special stains for decking which are designed to withstand a lot of wear and tear. Here, I have chosen a slightly blue-green with grey and blue-grey for the balustrades.

Where water goes under a deck it is especially important to use products which will not wash down and poison the water.

Plants

Apart from climbers on the wall and pergola, there are plenty of deep soil borders – generally a much better option than having to rely entirely on pots. Small shrubs like cistus, purple sage, santolina, and *Hebe* 'Mrs Winder' have been used alongside phormium, irises and various other herbaceous flowers to produce a colourful display. The wooden trough can be used for seasonal flowers and the pond surround for dwarf ornamental grasses and creeping perenni-

als. Fragrance can come from climbers like summer jasmine and honeysuckle as well as from lilies, stocks and aromatic herbs grown in pots.

A deck can be easily made to feel like an outdoor room especially on warm summer evenings when subtle lighting will bring it alive and lift it from the darkness of the surrounding garden.

APPENDIX
Pump sizes for water features

Calculating the capacity of a pond

Length x width x maximum depth of the pond (in metres) x 1000 gives the capacity in litres.

Calculating a pump for filtering

The pump should be capable of circulating *all* the water in the pond every two hours. For example, a pond holding 2000 litres of water will need a pump capacity of 1000 litres per hour.

The head

This is the height, above the surface of the lowest pool or reservoir, to which the pump will have to raise water (assuming that the pump is housed within the lowest pool). All pump performance tables include a column showing the head.

Waterfalls

A good flow for a waterfall 15cm (6in) wide is about 1500 litres per hour. Choose a pump which can easily deliver this to the required height (head), *plus 25%* to allow for friction in pipes and eventual deterioration due to debris. A waterfall twice as wide will need a pump twice as powerful. As a general rule, always choose a pump that is more powerful than required, and incorporate a flow valve. This will help to ensure that there is always an appropriate volume of water.

Fountains

These are very variable but, in terms of height, should never be higher than the radius of the pool (i.e. half its diameter), so that water is not lost on a windy day. Based on this, as a rough guide, a pond containing up to 2000 litres of water will probably require a pump output of about 1000 litres per hour. For further information, see the articles in the 'Practicalities' section.

ABOUT THE AUTHOR

Roger Sweetinburgh was born in 1945. Although neither of his parents came from a horticultural background, they enjoyed tending their small suburban garden, which is where Roger's interest first started.

He was always trying out new ideas and growing various plants in a cold frame which he had built in after-school woodwork classes. Once school days were over, he wasted no time in joining a full-time course at the local horticultural college.

His determination to work in as many different branches of horticulture as possible led him into becoming a landscape contractor, a nurseryman, a quality control officer, a senior parks officer and a full-time lecturer in landscape construction back at the college where he first started. It was while lecturing that he developed a special interest in garden design; he eventually gave up his lecturing job to become a full-time freelance garden designer. Since then, he has designed literally thousands of gardens around Britain and abroad, as well as writing and illustrating several books on the subject.

Photographic credits

Arcadian Garden Features Ltd:
page 17

Brian Bevan:
pages 45, 46, 48

Fred Downham:
page 12 (bottom)

Michael Edwards:
page 69

GMC Publications/Anthony Bailey:
page 26

GMC Publications/Graham Clarke:
pages 21, 104 (top left and bottom right), 112, 115

GMC Publications/Ed Gabriel:
cover; opposite page 1; pages 2-3, 13, 59, 68, 73, 77, 81, 83, 87, 101 (top right and centre), 105

GMC Publications/Andrea Hargreaves:
page 85

GMC Publications/Christine Richardson:
page 25

GMC Publications/Chris Skarbon:
frontispiece; pages 20 (right), 36-7, 49, 60-1, 67

HL Photographics:
pages 9 (top right), 12 (top)

Nigel Phillips:
page 66

Harry Smith Horticultural Photographic Collection:
pages 8-9, 12 (centre), 31-5, 40, 41, 52, 54-6, 58, 74-6, 79, 91-3, 100, 101 (top left and bottom), 104 (bottom left), 109

Roger Sweetinburgh:
pages 96, 97, 99

Geoff Whiten:
page 107

INDEX

TITLES AVAILABLE FROM
GMC Publications
BOOKS

GARDENING

Auriculas for Everyone: How to Grow and Show Perfect Plants
Mary Robinson

Beginners' Guide to Herb Gardening — *Yvonne Cuthbertson*
Beginners' Guide to Water Gardening — *Graham Clarke*
Bird Boxes and Feeders for the Garden — *Dave Mackenzie*
The Birdwatcher's Garden — *Hazel & Pamela Johnson*
Broad-Leaved Evergreens — *Stephen G. Haw*
Companions to Clematis: Growing Clematis with Other Plants
Marigold Badcock

Creating Contrast with Dark Plants — *Freya Martin*
Creating Small Habitats for Wildlife in your Garden — *Josie Briggs*
Exotics are Easy — *GMC Publications*
Gardening with Hebes — *Chris & Valerie Wheeler*
Gardening with Wild Plants — *Julian Slatcher*
Growing Cacti and Other Succulents in the Conservatory and Indoors
Shirley-Anne Bell

Growing Cacti and Other Succulents in the Garden — *Shirley-Anne Bell*
Hardy Perennials: A Beginner's Guide — *Eric Sawford*
Hedges: Creating Screens and Edges — *Averil Bedrich*
The Living Tropical Greenhouse: Creating a Haven for Butterflies
John & Maureen Tampion

Marginal Plants — *Bernard Sleeman*
Orchids are Easy: A Beginner's Guide to their Care and Cultivation
Tom Gilland

Plant Alert: A Garden Guide for Parents — *Catherine Collins*
Planting Plans for Your Garden — *Jenny Shukman*
Plants that Span the Seasons — *Roger Wilson*
Sink and Container Gardening Using Dwarf Hardy Plants
Chris & Valerie Wheeler

The Successful Conservatory and Growing Exotic Plants — *Joan Phelan*
Tropical Garden Style with Hardy Plants — *Alan Hemsley*
Water Garden Projects: From Groundwork to Planting
Roger Sweetinburgh

CRAFTS

American Patchwork Designs in Needlepoint — *Melanie Tacon*
A Beginners' Guide to Rubber Stamping — *Brenda Hunt*
Beginning Picture Marquetry — *Lawrence Threadgold*
Blackwork: A New Approach — *Brenda Day*
Celtic Cross Stitch Designs — *Carol Phillipson*
Celtic Knotwork Designs — *Sheila Sturrock*
Celtic Knotwork Handbook — *Sheila Sturrock*
Celtic Spirals and Other Designs — *Sheila Sturrock*
Complete Pyrography — *Stephen Poole*
Creative Backstitch — *Helen Hall*
Creative Embroidery Techniques Using Colour Through Gold
Daphne J. Ashby & Jackie Woolsey

The Creative Quilter: Techniques and Projects — *Pauline Brown*
Cross-Stitch Designs from China — *Carol Phillipson*
Decoration on Fabric: A Sourcebook of Ideas — *Pauline Brown*
Decorative Beaded Purses — *Enid Taylor*
Designing and Making Cards — *Glennis Gilruth*
Glass Engraving Pattern Book — *John Everett*
Glass Painting — *Emma Sedman*
Handcrafted Rugs — *Sandra Hardy*
How to Arrange Flowers: A Japanese Approach to English Design
Taeko Marvelly

How to Make First-Class Cards — *Debbie Brown*
An Introduction to Crewel Embroidery — *Mave Glenny*
Making and Using Working Drawings for Realistic Model Animals
Basil F. Fordham

Making Character Bears — *Valerie Tyler*
Making Decorative Screens — *Amanda Howes*
Making Fabergé-Style Eggs — *Denise Hopper*
Making Fairies and Fantastical Creatures — *Julie Sharp*
Making Greetings Cards for Beginners — *Pat Sutherland*
Making Hand-Sewn Boxes: Techniques and Projects — *Jackie Woolsey*
Making Knitwear Fit — *Pat Ashforth & Steve Plummer*
Making Mini Cards, Gift Tags & Invitations — *Glennis Gilruth*
Making Soft-Bodied Dough Characters — *Patricia Hughes*
Natural Ideas for Christmas: Fantastic Decorations to Make
Josie Cameron-Ashcroft & Carol Cox

New Ideas for Crochet: Stylish Projects for the Home — *Darsha Capaldi*
Papercraft Projects for Special Occasions — *Sine Chesterman*
Patchwork for Beginners — *Pauline Brown*
Pyrography Designs — *Norma Gregory*
Pyrography Handbook (Practical Crafts) — *Stephen Poole*
Rose Windows for Quilters — *Angela Besley*
Rubber Stamping with Other Crafts — *Lynne Garner*
Sponge Painting — *Ann Rooney*
Stained Glass: Techniques and Projects — *Mary Shanahan*
Step-by-Step Pyrography Projects for the Solid Point Machine
Norma Gregory

Tassel Making for Beginners — *Enid Taylor*
Tatting Collage — *Lindsay Rogers*
Tatting Patterns — *Lyn Morton*
Temari: A Traditional Japanese Embroidery Technique — *Margaret Ludlow*
Trip Around the World: 25 Patchwork, Quilting and Appliqué Projects
Gail Lawther

Trompe l'Oeil: Techniques and Projects — *Jan Lee Johnson*
Tudor Treasures to Embroider — *Pamela Warner*
Wax Art — *Hazel Marsh*

WOODCARVING

Beginning Woodcarving — *GMC Publications*
Carving Architectural Detail in Wood: The Classical Tradition
Frederick Wilbur

Carving Birds & Beasts — *GMC Publications*
Carving the Human Figure: Studies in Wood and Stone — *Dick Onians*
Carving Nature: Wildlife Studies in Wood — *Frank Fox-Wilson*
Carving on Turning — *Chris Pye*
Decorative Woodcarving — *Jeremy Williams*
Elements of Woodcarving — *Chris Pye*
Essential Woodcarving Techniques — *Dick Onians*
Lettercarving in Wood: A Practical Course — *Chris Pye*
Making & Using Working Drawings for Realistic Model Animals
Basil F. Fordham

Power Tools for Woodcarving — *David Tippey*
Relief Carving in Wood: A Practical Introduction — *Chris Pye*
Understanding Woodcarving in the Round — *GMC Publications*
Useful Techniques for Woodcarvers — *GMC Publications*
Woodcarving: A Foundation Course — *Zoë Gertner*
Woodcarving for Beginners — *GMC Publications*
Woodcarving Tools, Materials & Equipment (New Edition in 2 vols.)
Chris Pye

WOODTURNING

Adventures in Woodturning — *David Springett*
Bert Marsh: Woodturner — *Bert Marsh*
Bowl Turning Techniques Masterclass — *Tony Boase*
Chris Child's Projects for Woodturners — *Chris Child*
Colouring Techniques for Woodturners — *Jan Sanders*
Contemporary Turned Wood: New Perspectives in a Rich Tradition — *Ray Leier, Jan Peters & Kevin Wallace*
The Craftsman Woodturner — *Peter Child*
Decorating Turned Wood: The Maker's Eye — *Liz & Michael O'Donnell*
Decorative Techniques for Woodturners — *Hilary Bowen*
Illustrated Woodturning Techniques — *John Hunnex*
Intermediate Woodturning Projects — *GMC Publications*
Keith Rowley's Woodturning Projects — *Keith Rowley*
Making Screw Threads in Wood — *Fred Holder*
Turned Boxes: 50 Designs — *Chris Stott*
Turning Green Wood — *Michael O'Donnell*
Turning Pens and Pencils — *Kip Christensen & Rex Burningham*
Useful Woodturning Projects — *GMC Publications*
Woodturning: Bowls, Platters, Hollow Forms, Vases, Vessels, Bottles, Flasks, Tankards, Plates — *GMC Publications*
Woodturning: A Foundation Course (New Edition) — *Keith Rowley*
Woodturning: A Fresh Approach — *Robert Chapman*
Woodturning: An Individual Approach — *Dave Regester*
Woodturning: A Source Book of Shapes — *John Hunnex*
Woodturning Jewellery — *Hilary Bowen*
Woodturning Masterclass — *Tony Boase*
Woodturning Techniques — *GMC Publications*

WOODWORKING

Advanced Scrollsaw Projects — *GMC Publications*
Beginning Picture Marquetry — *Lawrence Threadgold*
Bird Boxes and Feeders for the Garden — *Dave Mackenzie*
Celtic Carved Lovespoons: 30 Patterns — *Sharon Littley & Clive Griffin*
Celtic Woodcraft — *Glenda Bennett*
Complete Woodfinishing — *Ian Hosker*
David Charlesworth's Furniture-Making Techniques — *David Charlesworth*
David Charlesworth's Furniture-Making Techniques – Volume 2 — *David Charlesworth*
The Encyclopedia of Joint Making — *Terrie Noll*
Furniture-Making Projects for the Wood Craftsman — *GMC Publications*
Furniture-Making Techniques for the Wood Craftsman — *GMC Publications*
Furniture Restoration (Practical Crafts) — *Kevin Jan Bonner*
Furniture Restoration: A Professional at Work — *John Lloyd*
Furniture Restoration and Repair for Beginners — *Kevin Jan Bonner*
Furniture Restoration Workshop — *Kevin Jan Bonner*
Green Woodwork — *Mike Abbott*
Intarsia: 30 Patterns for the Scrollsaw — *John Everett*
Kevin Ley's Furniture Projects — *Kevin Ley*
Making Chairs and Tables — *GMC Publications*
Making Chairs and Tables – Volume 2 — *GMC Publications*
Making Classic English Furniture — *Paul Richardson*
Making Heirloom Boxes — *Peter Lloyd*
Making Little Boxes from Wood — *John Bennett*
Making Screw Threads in Wood — *Fred Holder*
Making Shaker Furniture — *Barry Jackson*
Making Woodwork Aids and Devices — *Robert Wearing*
Mastering the Router — *Ron Fox*
Pine Furniture Projects for the Home — *Dave Mackenzie*
Practical Scrollsaw Patterns — *John Everett*
Router Magic: Jigs, Fixtures and Tricks to Unleash your Router's Full Potential — *Bill Hylton*
Router Tips & Techniques — *Robert Wearing*
Routing: A Workshop Handbook — *Anthony Bailey*
Routing for Beginners — *Anthony Bailey*

Sharpening: The Complete Guide — *Jim Kingshott*
Sharpening Pocket Reference Book — *Jim Kingshott*
Simple Scrollsaw Projects — *GMC Publications*
Space-Saving Furniture Projects — *Dave Mackenzie*
Stickmaking: A Complete Course — *Andrew Jones & Clive George*
Stickmaking Handbook — *Andrew Jones & Clive George*
Storage Projects for the Router — *GMC Publications*
Test Reports: The Router and Furniture & Cabinetmaking — *GMC Publications*
Veneering: A Complete Course — *Ian Hosker*
Veneering Handbook — *Ian Hosker*
Woodfinishing Handbook (Practical Crafts) — *Ian Hosker*
Woodworking with the Router: Professional Router Techniques any Woodworker can Use — *Bill Hylton & Fred Matlack*

UPHOLSTERY

The Upholsterer's Pocket Reference Book — *David James*
Upholstery: A Complete Course (Revised Edition) — *David James*
Upholstery Restoration — *David James*
Upholstery Techniques & Projects — *David James*
Upholstery Tips and Hints — *David James*

TOYMAKING

Scrollsaw Toy Projects — *Ivor Carlyle*
Scrollsaw Toys for All Ages — *Ivor Carlyle*

DOLLS' HOUSES AND MINIATURES

1/12 Scale Character Figures for the Dolls' House — *James Carrington*
Americana in 1/12 Scale: 50 Authentic Projects — *Joanne Ogreenc & Mary Lou Santovec*
Architecture for Dolls' Houses — *Joyce Percival*
The Authentic Georgian Dolls' House — *Brian Long*
A Beginners' Guide to the Dolls' House Hobby — *Jean Nisbett*
Celtic, Medieval and Tudor Wall Hangings in 1/12 Scale Needlepoint — *Sandra Whitehead*
Creating Decorative Fabrics: Projects in 1/12 Scale — *Janet Storey*
The Dolls' House 1/24 Scale: A Complete Introduction — *Jean Nisbett*
Dolls' House Accessories, Fixtures and Fittings — *Andrea Barham*
Dolls' House Furniture: Easy-to-Make Projects in 1/12 Scale — *Freida Gray*
Dolls' House Makeovers — *Jean Nisbett*
Dolls' House Window Treatments — *Eve Harwood*
Easy to Make Dolls' House Accessories — *Andrea Barham*
Edwardian-Style Hand-Knitted Fashion for 1/12 Scale Dolls — *Yvonne Wakefield*
How to Make Your Dolls' House Special: Fresh Ideas for Decorating — *Beryl Armstrong*
Make Your Own Dolls' House Furniture — *Maurice Harper*
Making Dolls' House Furniture — *Patricia King*
Making Georgian Dolls' Houses — *Derek Rowbottom*
Making Miniature Chinese Rugs and Carpets — *Carol Phillipson*
Making Miniature Food and Market Stalls — *Angie Scarr*
Making Miniature Gardens — *Freida Gray*
Making Miniature Oriental Rugs & Carpets — *Meik & Ian McNaughton*
Making Period Dolls' House Accessories — *Andrea Barham*
Making Tudor Dolls' Houses — *Derek Rowbottom*
Making Victorian Dolls' House Furniture — *Patricia King*
Miniature Bobbin Lace — *Roz Snowden*
Miniature Embroidery for the Georgian Dolls' House — *Pamela Warner*
Miniature Embroidery for the Tudor and Stuart Dolls' House — *Pamela Warner*
Miniature Embroidery for the Victorian Dolls' House — *Pamela Warner*
Miniature Needlepoint Carpets — *Janet Granger*
More Miniature Oriental Rugs & Carpets — *Meik & Ian McNaughton*
Needlepoint 1/12 Scale: Design Collections for the Dolls' House — *Felicity Price*
New Ideas for Miniature Bobbin Lace — *Roz Snowden*
The Secrets of the Dolls' House Makers — *Jean Nisbett*

PHOTOGRAPHY

Close-Up on Insects	*Robert Thompson*
An Essential Guide to Bird Photography	*Steve Young*
Field Guide to Landscape Photography	*Peter Watson*
How to Photograph Pets	*Nick Ridley*
Light in the Landscape: A Photographer's Year	*Peter Watson*
Outdoor Photography Portfolio	*GMC Publications*
Photographing Fungi in the Field	*George McCarthy*
Photography for the Naturalist	*Mark Lucock*
Viewpoints from *Outdoor Photography*	*GMC Publications*
Where and How to Photograph Wildlife	*Peter Evans*
Wild Life: A Photographer's Year	*Andy Rouse*

ART TECHNIQUES

Oil Paintings from your Garden: A Guide for Beginners	*Rachel Shirley*

VIDEOS

Drop-in and Pinstuffed Seats	*David James*
Stuffover Upholstery	*David James*
Elliptical Turning	*David Springett*
Woodturning Wizardry	*David Springett*
Turning Between Centres: The Basics	*Dennis White*
Turning Bowls	*Dennis White*
Boxes, Goblets and Screw Threads	*Dennis White*
Novelties and Projects	*Dennis White*
Classic Profiles	*Dennis White*
Twists and Advanced Turning	*Dennis White*
Sharpening the Professional Way	*Jim Kingshott*
Sharpening Turning & Carving Tools	*Jim Kingshott*
Bowl Turning	*John Jordan*
Hollow Turning	*John Jordan*
Woodturning: A Foundation Course	*Keith Rowley*
Carving a Figure: The Female Form	*Ray Gonzalez*
The Router: A Beginner's Guide	*Alan Goodsell*
The Scroll Saw: A Beginner's Guide	*John Burke*

MAGAZINES

WOODTURNING ✦ WOODCARVING ✦ FURNITURE & CABINETMAKING
THE ROUTER ✦ NEW WOODWORKING ✦ THE DOLLS' HOUSE MAGAZINE
OUTDOOR PHOTOGRAPHY ✦ BLACK & WHITE PHOTOGRAPHY
MACHINE KNITTING NEWS ✦ BUSINESSMATTERS

The above represents a full list of all titles currently published or scheduled to be published.
All are available direct from the Publishers or through bookshops, newsagents and specialist retailers.
To place an order, or to obtain a complete catalogue, contact:

**GMC Publications,
Castle Place, 166 High Street, Lewes, East Sussex BN7 1XU, United Kingdom
Tel: 01273 488005 Fax: 01273 478606
E-mail: pubs@thegmcgroup.com**

Orders by credit card are accepted